CHICAGO
CATHOLIC CHURCHES

CHICAGO
CATHOLIC CHURCHES

A Sketchbook

HARRISON FILLMORE

Foreword by Father Thomas Nangle

Published by The History Press
Charleston, SC
www.historypress.com

Copyright © 2022 by Harrison Fillmore
All rights reserved

First published 2022

Manufactured in the United States

ISBN 9781467151726

Library of Congress Control Number: 2021950643

Notice: The information in this book is true and complete to the best of our knowledge. It is offered without guarantee on the part of the author or The History Press. The author and The History Press disclaim all liability in connection with the use of this book.

All rights reserved. No part of this book may be reproduced or transmitted in any form whatsoever without prior written permission from the publisher except in the case of brief quotations embodied in critical articles and reviews.

A portion of the proceeds goes to the Chicago Police Department Chaplain's Ministry and the Gold Star families.

CONTENTS

Foreword, by Father Thomas Nangle	17
Angel Guardian	19
St. Mary of the Assumption	20
St. Mary (Colonial)	20
St. Mary (Plymouth)	21
St. Mary (Chapel)	21
New "Old" St. Mary (Modern)	21
Holy Name Cathedral	22
St. James Chapel	22
St. Peter	23
St. Wenceslaus	23
Assumption	24
St. Patrick (Old St. Pat's)	25
Notre Dame	27
St. Philip Benizi	28
San Marcello Mission	28
St. Joseph	29
St. Dominic	29
Immaculate Conception	30
St. Michael (Old Town)	31
St. James	32
St. John	33

Contents

St. Adalbert	33
St. Joseph (Pilsen)	34
Providence of God	34
Holy Trinity (Croatian)	35
St. Anne (Pilsen)	35
St. Procopius	36
Sacred Heart (Pilsen)	36
St. Paul	37
St. Stephen	38
St. Pius V	38
St. Vitus	39
Our Lady of Tepeyac	39
Assumption (24th and California)	40
Blessed Sacrament	40
Epiphany	41
Good Shepherd	42
Our Lady of Vilna	42
St. Therese Chinese	42
St. Roman	43
St. Ludmilla	43
St. Michael the Archangel	43
All Saints–St. Anthony	44
All Saints (Original)	45
St. Barbara	45
St. Agnes of Bohemia	46
St. Jerome (Croatian)	47
St. Bridget	47
St. Lucia	47
St. John Nepoceme	48
Monastery of the Holy Cross	48
St. Mary of Perpetual Help	49
St. David	50
St. George	50
Our Lady of Good Counsel	50
St. Maurice	51
St. Monica	51
Nativity of Our Lord	51
Ss. Peter and Paul	52
St. Joseph/St. Anne	52

Contents

St. George	53
St. Agnes	53
Holy Angels	54
St. Elizabeth	54
St. Gabriel	55
St. Cecelia	56
Immaculate Heart of Mary Vicariate	56
Holy Cross	57
Sacred Heart of Jesus	59
St. Ambrose	59
St. Rose of Lima	59
St. Michael the Archangel	60
St. Joseph (Shrine of)	60
Corpus Christi	61
St. Cyril and Methodius	61
St. John the Baptist	62
St. Augustine	63
St. Basil	63
St. Anne	64
St. Charles Lwanga	64
Visitation	65
St. John of God	66
St. Raphael	66
St. Martin	67
St. Thomas the Apostle	68
Assumption BVM	68
St. Anselm	69
St. Theodore	69
Our Lady of Solace	70
St. Rita of Cascia	70
St. Clara–St. Gelasius	71
St. Bernard	71
Holy Cross	72
St. Benedict the African	72
St. Brendan	73
St. Justin Martyr	74
St. Columbanus	74
St. Philip Neri	75
St. Laurence	75

Contents

St. Carthage	76
St. Bride	76
St. Leo the Great	76
St. Francis DePaula	77
St. Dorothy	77
St. Sabina	77
Our Lady of Peace	78
St. Therese of the Infant Jesus	79
St. Bronislava	79
St. Michael	80
St. Mary Magdalene	81
St. Felicitas	81
St. Clotilde	81
St. Kilian	82
St. John Baptist	82
St. Joseph	82
Immaculate Conception	83
St. Ethelreda	84
St. Ailbe	84
St. Joachim	85
Ss. Peter and Paul	85
Our Lady of Guadalupe	86
Our Lady of Hungary	86
St. Patrick	87
St. George	87
Sacred Heart	87
Our Lady Gate of Heaven	88
St. Thaddeus	88
St. Helena of the Cross	88
St. John De La Salle	89
St. Kevin	89
St. Francis De Sales	89
Holy Rosary	90
All Saints	90
Annunciata	90
Holy Name of Mary	91
St. Willibrord	91
Sacred Heart (Mission of Holy Name of Mary)	91
Holy Rosary	92

Contents

St. Anthony	94
St. Louis De France	94
St. Salomea	95
St. Catherine of Genoa	97
Assumption BVM (Closed)	97
Ss. Peter and Paul	97
St. Florian	98
St. Nicholas	98
Our Lady of the Gardens	98
St. Columba	99
St. Mary of the Assumption	99
St. Walter	99
St. Cajetan	100
St. Christina	100
St. John Fisher	100
St. Barnabas	101
St. Margaret of Scotland	101
Christ the King	102
St. Thomas More	102
St. Bede the Venerable	102
St. Denis	103
Queen of the Universe	103
St. Adrian	103
Nativity BVM	104
St. Mary of Mount Carmel	104
St. Mary Star of the Sea	105
St. Rene Goupil	105
St. Symphorosa and Her Seven Sons	105
St. Nicholas of Tolentine	106
St. Tiribius	106
St. Gall	106
St. Clare Montefalco	107
St. Camillus	107
St. Daniel the Prophet	108
St. Jane de Chantel	108
St. Simon the Apostle	109
St. Richard	109
St. Bruno	110
Our Lady of Snows	110

Contents

Immaculate Conception	111
St. Pancratius	111
Five Holy Martyrs	112
Holy Innocents	112
Holy Guardian Angel	113
Our Lady of Good Counsel	113
St. Stephen King of Hungary	113
Holy Family	114
St. John Cantius	115
St. Mary of the Angels	117
St. Stephen	118
St. Matthew	118
Our Lady of Sorrows Basilica	119
St. Jarlath	120
Our Lady of Pompeii	120
Presentation	121
Our Lady of Angels	121
Holy Rosary	122
Our Lady Help of Christians	122
Our Lady of Lourdes	123
St. Francis Assisi	123
Santa Maria Addolorata	123
St. Finbarr	124
Holy Trinity	124
St. Malachy	125
Sacred Heart	126
Precious Blood	126
St. Columbkille	127
St. Frances Xavier Cabrini	127
Resurrection	128
St. Cyril and Methodius	128
St. Francis Assisi	128
St. Thomas Aquinas	129
St. Angela	130
St. Lucy	131
St. Peter Canisius	131
Holy Ghost	131
St. Mel	132
St. Agatha	133

Contents

St. Charles Borromeo	134
St. Callistus	134
Maternity BVM	134
St. William of Vercelli	135
St. Francis Borgia	135
St. James the Apostle	136
St. Ferdinand	136
St. Priscilla	137
St. Constance	137
St. Wenceslaus	138
St. Veronica	138
St. Sylvester	139
Christ the Redeemer Belarusian	140
St. Hedwig Mission	140
Our Lady of Grace	141
St. John Berchman	142
St. Genevieve	142
Our Lady of Mercy	143
St. Hyacinth Mission	143
St. Mark	144
Resurrection	144
St. Fidelis	145
Annunciation	145
St. Helen	145
St. Aloysius	146
St. Hyacinth	147
St. Philomena	148
St. John Bosco	148
St. Ladislaus	149
St. Mary of Providence	149
Our Lady of Agnola	150
St. Stanislaus Bishop and Martyr	150
St. Stanislaus Kostka	151
St. Boniface	152
Holy Trinity	153
St. Hedwig	154
Our Lady of Victory	154
Immaculate Heart of Mary (North)	155
St. Sebastian	155

Contents

St. Vincent DePaul	156
St. Teresa	156
St. Josaphat	157
St. Clement	157
St. Frances Xavier Cabrini (National Shrine of)	158
St. Bonaventure	158
St. Alphonsus	159
Our Lady of Mount Carmel	160
St. Andrew	160
St. Benedict	161
Queen of Angels	162
St. Mary of the Lake	162
Our Lady of Lourdes	163
St. Thomas Canterbury	163
St. Ita	164
St. Gertrude	165
St. Gregory	167
St. Matthias	167
Madonna Della Strada	168
St. Margaret Mary	168
Our Lady of the Cross Mission	169
St. Henry	169
St. Ignatius	169
St. Timothy	170
St. Jerome	170
St. Pascal	171
Our Lady of Mother of Church	172
Shrine of the Sacred Heart	172
St. Bartholomew	173
Korean Martyrs Catholic Church	173
St. Viator	174
St. Edward	174
St. Eugene	175
St. Cornelius	175
Transfiguration of Our Lord	176
St. Hilary	176
St. Robert Bellarmine	177
St. Monica	177
Immaculate Conception	178

Contents

St. Tarcissus	179
St. Thecla	179
St. Juliana	180
St. Mary of the Woods	180
Queen of All Saints	181
Bibliography	183
Index	185
About the Author	191

FOREWORD

You're on vacation. You're from Chicago. You spot someone wearing a T-shirt with "Chicago" on it. You say, "Hi, me too, South Side. How about you?"

"Vis," she says, and you say, "CK for me." And the connection is made. It is a (dying) Chicago custom to answer "where are you from?" by naming your Catholic parish rather than your neighborhood or major streets. So "Vis" is Visitation and "CK" is Christ the King. Sometimes our Protestant or Jewish friends would use the same geographic shorthand in a friendly, good-natured interfaith nod to a Catholic custom. And we'd all smile.

A church burns down. If the pastor is an administrator, he will think immediately in terms of money, insurance and a long, long fundraiser. And if the pastor is a good shepherd, he will think in terms of, "It's only a building." So wise and so true. The church is the people. But buildings can have souls. People go to a church to be more aware of God, even though God doesn't live there. But they want to rub souls with God or others in their family of faith. The church building holds those intimacies and connections, and along with the decades-old essences of incense and beeswax smoke, varnish, flowers, stone and wood, it holds the tears and smiles of worry and relief, desperation and trust, weddings and funerals, sin and virtue, despair and hope, abandonment and gratitude, isolation and love, birth and death and every fire-and-ice moment in between. It holds the juice of human lives, from beginning to end.

Foreword

Driving west on Jackson Boulevard one morning about thirty years ago, I found myself in the 5000 block, and my eyes moved to the right to touch base with the front of Resurrection Church. It wasn't there. I actually became a little bit disoriented and wondered if I was on the wrong street and went around the block in disbelief because it appeared that the big stone church was gone. I pulled up and looked at the empty, rubble-strewn lot where the church that was so important in my family's history had stood. Indeed, it was gone. I was upset. I put the car back in gear and continued west, but I felt a bit unmoored and mildly betrayed, sad and nostalgic, angry and wondering, all jumbled together. It was only a building, yes. But it held so many memories of birth and death and everything in between for me and my family. The big old gray place had a soul.

A good street cop has exceptional eyes for details and dynamics. That skill keeps them alive on their ever-changing street encounters. The author/artist of this book has coupled his eye for detail with his skill at sketching to bring us uncomplicated drawings of some Chicago Catholic churches. As I paged through them, memories were tickled to life. Some were sweet, some funny, some deep, some happy and warm, some evoked rich memories and one was disturbing.

When folks say, "It's only a building" without affirming and recognizing its soul, it's like saying the American flag is only a piece of cloth, like a baby is only a little human being, like a symphony is only a collection of sounds, like a kitten is just a young cat, like America is just a bunch of states. It's only a building, but it holds the human histories of the souls that make up the real Church, God's family in faith.

—Father Thomas Nangle
Chicago Police Department
Chaplain, retired

A Sketchbook

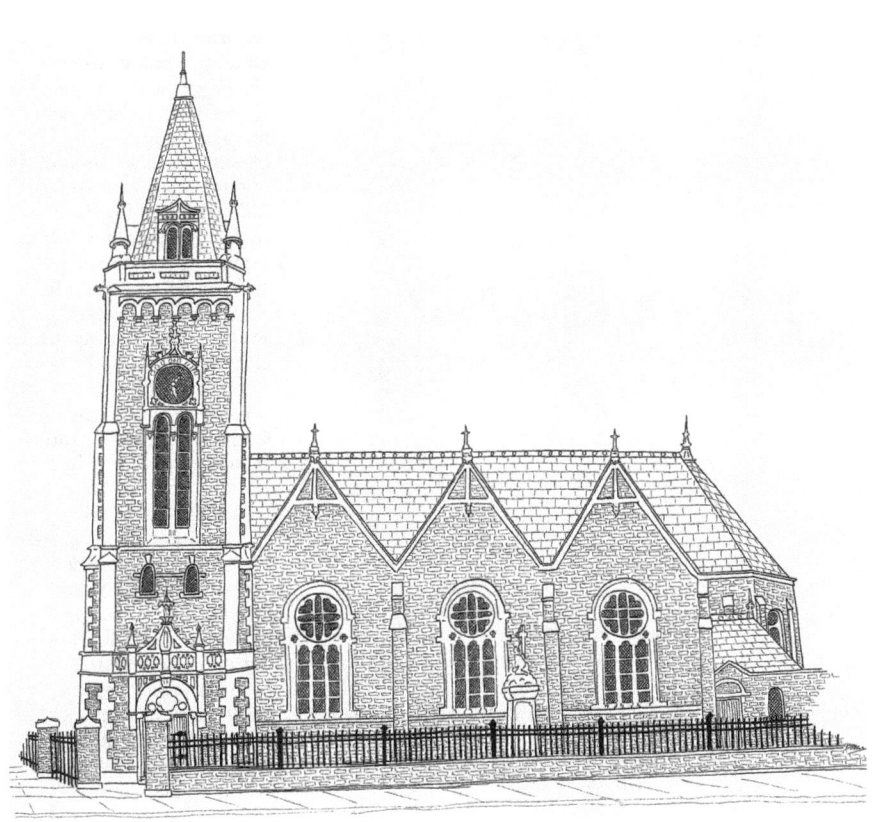

ANGEL GUARDIAN

Like many a family history, mine begins as a story of immigration. My family's Chicago history begins here, on the steps of Angel Guardian Church, where my grandmother's feet stood after being dropped off to live at the orphanage by her father so that he might return to the "old country" to work, save and bring back her brothers and sisters.

The parish was established by German immigrants in 1866 and was originally called St. Henry's. This Gothic church was built in 1906, and a school was built nearby. In 1929, the church was renamed Angel Guardian to match the attached orphanage, and St. Henry's Church moved to the first floor of the school building. Chicago's neighborhood ethnic demographics are constantly changing, and in 1972, the church served a new wave of immigrants and became the Blessed Aloysius Stepinac Croatian Catholic Church.

Chicago Catholic Churches

TOP **ST. MARY OF THE ASSUMPTION**
Chicago's first European visitor was Catholic priest Father Jacques Marquette in 1673. Impressed by his surroundings, he was quoted as saying, "We have seen nothing like this river we enter as regards its fertility of soil, its prairies and woods; its cattle, elk, deer, wildcats, bustards, swans, ducks, parroquats and even beaver."

Father Marquette was followed by many Catholics, including Father François Pinet, who in 1696 would found the Angel Guardian Mission. Later still, Jean Baptiste Point du Sable, a Black pioneer and Roman Catholic, would arrive, being recognized as the city's very first permanent resident.

But it wasn't until 1833 that Chicago saw the formation of its first parish, St. Mary of the Assumption. The very first mass was held in a building close to Billy Caldwell's Sauganash Tavern until a rudimentary wooden structure was built near Lake and State Streets.

BOTTOM **ST. MARY (COLONIAL)**
In 1842, a new St. Mary Church was built in an American Colonial style on the northwest corner of Madison Street and Wabash Avenue. That church was destroyed in the Chicago Fire.

A Sketchbook

TOP **ST. MARY (PLYMOUTH)** After several temporary structures, the archdiocese purchased the former Plymouth Congregational Church at 9th Street and Wabash Avenue. The Gothic church was the new home for St. Mary's. In 1970, that structure was razed to make way for a Standard Oil parking lot.

MIDDLE **ST. MARY (CHAPEL)** The parish worshiped for a time in this small chapel, and their numbers diminished in the south Loop.

BOTTOM **NEW "OLD" ST. MARY (MODERN)** The parish began to grow again as residents returned to the south Loop. Construction began on the new "old" St. Mary's, designed by Serena Sturm Architects, and it was completed in 2002. The new "old" St. Mary is an Ultra-Modern structure on the corner of 15th and Michigan.

Chicago Catholic Churches

TOP **HOLY NAME CATHEDRAL**
The Holy Name Parish was established in 1849. St. Mary's was the first official cathedral in Chicago, although locals regarded Holy Name as such. The original brick structure was destroyed in the Chicago Fire, and for a short period parishioners worshiped in a "shanty Cathedral," which was a repurposed, burnt-out and boarded-up building. This Victorian Gothic church, designed by architect Patrick Charles Kelly, was rebuilt and rededicated in 1875. If you look closely, on the corner of State and Superior you'll see bullet scars from Al Capone rival Dean O'Banion's murder.

BOTTOM **ST. JAMES CHAPEL**
Built in 1919, this French Gothic Revival structure at 835 North Rush is easy to miss in Chicago's crowded Gold Coast neighborhood. The chapel served the students of Quigley Prep Seminary until 2007, but it continues to thrive, serving the nearby archdiocese clergy and employees.

A Sketchbook

TOP **ST. PETER**
Called "a house of God in a valley of stone," this Modern Gothic church built in 1953 at 110 West Madison sits in the middle of the Loop. The parish was established by Germans in 1846, and a church was built at Franklin and Washington. The building was lost in the Chicago Fire. A new structure was built at Clark and Polk, but as conditions worsened, that church was closed and razed, making way for the construction of this final structure.

BOTTOM **ST. WENCESLAUS**
Chicago's first Bohemians established this church in 1863. The church at Dekoven and Desplaines was neighbor to Mrs. O'Leary's famous cow and the flashpoint of the Chicago Fire. This church was closed and demolished in 1955.

ASSUMPTION
Founded in 1881 and built in 1886, this Renaissance church at 319 West Illinois Street was the first to hold masses in Italian. Legend has it that Al Capone would hand out Easter baskets to the parishioners here.

ST. PATRICK (OLD ST. PAT'S)
This building is Romanesque with Celtic influence, specifically the Irish book of Kells. Considered now to be the oldest church in Chicago, the parish was organized in 1846 and the church was built in 1856. The church was one of the very few structures that survived the Chicago Fire and is today referred to as "Old" St. Pat's.

The heart and center of Chicago is the huge pile of masonry which reminds the visitor by its polished granite pillars and general massive and somber grandeur of the cathedrals and palaces of St. Petersburg.

—*William T. Stead,* If Christ Came to Chicago

A Sketchbook

NOTRE DAME
The original church—built by the French Catholics in their parish established in 1865—was destroyed in the Chicago Fire. This church, designed by architect Gregoire Vigeant, was built in 1887. This Romanesque Revival structure is located at 1336 West Flournoy in a neighborhood now known as Little Italy.

TOP **ST. PHILIP BENIZI**
This church, built in 1904 at Oak Street and Cambridge, was originally a mission of the Near North Side Italian Catholic Assumption Church. It became its own parish in 1915. The neighborhood known as Little Sicily changed, and the church was closed and razed in 1965.

BOTTOM **SAN MARCELLO MISSION**
Originally built as St. John, an Evangelist Episcopalian church at 517 West Evergreen, this church later became the San Marcello Mission in 1927. The church is known for its mural *All of Mankind* by local artist William Walker. The pastor invited Walker to paint his church in 1972. The church closed in 1974 and was home to Strangers Home Missionary Baptist Church until that, too, closed.

A Sketchbook

TOP **ST. JOSEPH**
Established in 1846, the original church was destroyed in the Chicago Fire. The new church, at Hill Street and Orleans, was dedicated in 1878 and heavily modernized in 1956. St. Joseph was combined with the Near North Immaculate Conception in 2016.

BOTTOM **ST. DOMINIC**
Irish Catholics established this parish in 1904, and this Romanesque church at Locust and Sedgwick was built two years later. Centered in the neighborhood nicknamed "Little Hell," the church served a mostly Italian and Sicilian congregation until the neighborhood changed once again, becoming predominantly African American. The church closed in 1990 and was razed in 2015.

IMMACULATE CONCEPTION
The original church, established in 1859, was built to serve the English-speaking followers, mostly Irish, who did not wish to attend the nearby German St. Michael's Church. The church was destroyed in the Chicago Fire and rebuilt in 1874. That church was razed in 1957, and this Modernist structure was built at 1431 North Park Avenue.

A Sketchbook

ST. MICHAEL (OLD TOWN)
St. Michael, established in 1852, was named for the patron saint of its main financier, Michael Diversey, owner of the Diversey and Lill brewery. The Chicago Fire gutted the building, leaving only the walls and part of the tower, but the resilient community rebuilt the Gothic structure. It was rededicated in 1873.

ST. JAMES

The frame church located at 27th and Prairie was the home of the ninth parish established in the city and founded for the Irish workers in the nearby Carville neighborhood, which no longer exists. The parish was also known to serve Catholic Confederate prisoners held in the Camp Douglas prison during the Civil War. The Victorian Gothic church known as "Old" St. James was built in 1880 at 29th and Wabash. The church was gutted by a horrible fire and rebuilt in 1972, only to be razed in 2013. At one time, it was considered the "mother of the South Side parishes," having its mission churches St. Thomas the Apostle, St. Anne and St. Patrick (South), among others.

ABOVE **ST. JOHN**
The Gothic church known as "Old" St. John in the south Loop at 18th and Clark Streets was established in 1859 and closed and razed in 1962.

LEFT **ST. ADALBERT**
Built in 1914, this Roman Basilica–style church by architect Henry J. Schlacks is located at 1656 West 17th Street. The parish was established in 1874 to serve the Polish immigrants in Pilsen but closed in 2016, and the neighborhood has been trying to save the church ever since. Plans for a music school fell through, as did a $4 million deal to build condos. Meanwhile, there have been attempts to develop the church into one large bed-and-breakfast. As of this writing, there are no solid plans.

ST. JOSEPH (PILSEN)
St. Joseph church and school was a small Slovak parish located 730 West 17th Place. Established in 1906, it closed in 1968.

PROVIDENCE OF GOD
Established in 1900, the parish was founded as a mission to Bridgeport's St. George Lithuanian Church. This Romanesque Revival church at 18th Street and Union was built in 1914 to serve Lithuanians in East Pilsen. The parish recently merged with St. Procopius.

HOLY TRINITY (CROATIAN)
Established in 1914 as a mission of St. Jerome Croatian, the church was built at 1850 South Throop and closed in 1990. Masses continued through 2004 until the church merged with St. Procopius.

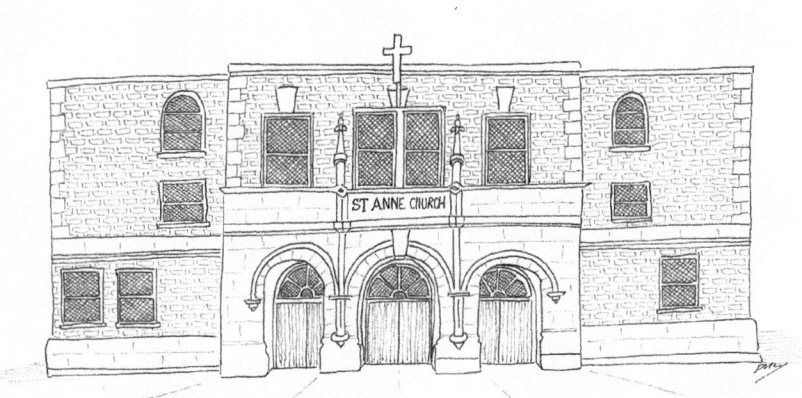

ST. ANNE (PILSEN)
This church and school combined was established in 1903 at 18th and Leavitt. Both officially closed in 2016, with the final mass in 2018.

Chicago Catholic Churches

TOP **ST. PROCOPIUS**
The Czech population of Pilsen established this parish in 1875. This Romanesque church was designed by architect P. Huber and built in 1883. St. Procopius College was founded here until it moved to the suburb of Lisle; it is now known as Illinois Benedictine College.

BOTTOM **SACRED HEART (PILSEN)**
Established in 1872, the parish of Sacred Heart in Pilsen at 19th Street and Peoria was originally a mission of Holy Family Church called St. Stanislaus. The church was built in 1875 and later closed and razed in 1959.

ST. PAUL
Old German craftsmanship built this Gothic church, known as the church "built without a nail." The parish was established in 1876, and the church, located at 22nd Place and Hoyne, was designed by architect Henry J. Schlacks and built in 1899.

TOP **ST. STEPHEN**
This Neo-Gothic church was established by west Pilsen Slovaks in 1898. The congregation took over this former Swedish church at 22nd Place and Wolcott. It is now part of the Cristo de Rey campus.

BOTTOM **ST. PIUS V**
Established in 1874 and built in 1885 at 19th and Ashland, this is the only Catholic church in the United States with Christopher Columbus on the main stained-glass window.

A Sketchbook

TOP **ST. VITUS**
Architects Kallal and Milotor designed this Romanesque church at 1820 South Paulina, built in 1897. The Czech church was closed in 1990 when it became a vibrant social work center.

BOTTOM
OUR LADY OF TEPEYAC
The parish was established in 1904 for the Polish and Lithuanians in the neighborhood. As the neighborhood demographics changed to mostly Catholic Mexicans, St. Ludmilla closed and merged on the site of St. Casimer at Cermak and Whipple Streets in 1990 to become Our Lady of Tepeyac church. In 2021, the church became part of the Mother of the Americas Parish.

Chicago Catholic Churches

TOP **ASSUMPTION (24TH AND CALIFORNIA)** The Mother of the Americas Parish is the new name of the combined churches of St. Roman, Our Lady of Tepeyac and Assumption in the Little Village neighborhood. This church, established in 1903, is set on the boulevard where Marshall turns into 24th Street near California Avenue.

BOTTOM **BLESSED SACRAMENT** This Romanesque church at Cermak and Central Park was closed in 2005 after merging with several local parishes. The church was utilized for different purposes and serves today as a Catholic Youth Center.

EPIPHANY
This parish was established by Bohemians in 1901, and this grand Neo-Gothic church was built in 1915 at 25th and Keeler. The parish merged with Good Shepherd in 2020.

Chicago Catholic Churches

TOP **GOOD SHEPHERD** Although this was originally territory of St. Casimir's, Polish Catholics established this parish in 1907. This Modernist functional church was built in 1968, and its very first mass was held on Christmas Day. The parish closed after merging with Epiphany in 2021.

MIDDLE **OUR LADY OF VILNA** This Lithuanian parish and school, located at 2323 West 23rd Street, was built in 1906. Known as Our Lady of Vilna in English, the Lithuanian translation is "Our Lady Gate of Dawn." It was closed in 1987 and recently served as a charter school.

BOTTOM **ST. THERESE CHINESE** Located at 218 West Alexander, this parish was established in the Chinatown neighborhood in 1947. It later took over the Italian Maria Incoronata Church in 1963 after that parish merged with the nearby Italian parish of St. Lucia.

A Sketchbook

TOP **ST. ROMAN**
This Romanesque Revival church at 23rd and Washtenaw, established in 1928 and built in 1929, originally served Chicago's Polish immigrants and later Mexican immigrants in the Little Village neighborhood. The parish closed in 1990 and finally merged with Mother of the Americas Parish in 2020.

MIDDLE **ST. LUDMILLA**
Established by Bohemian Catholics in 1891 at 24th and Albany, this church was closed after it merged with Our Lady of Tepeyac in 1990. The church was later demolished.

BOTTOM **ST. MICHAEL THE ARCHANGEL**
This tiny Italian parish, established in 1903, was located in the Heart of Chicago neighborhood near 24th and Oakley. Legend has it that the church was known to make bootleg sacramental wine in the basement during Prohibition. The parish was closed in 2003.

Chicago Catholic Churches

ALL SAINTS–ST. ANTHONY
This Romanesque church at 2849 South Wallace was designed by architect Henry J. Schlacks. It was built in 1915 as a combined parish after the merge of the Bridgeport parishes of All Saints (Irish, at 25th and Wallace) and St. Anthony of Padua (German, at 24th and Canal).

A Sketchbook

TOP **ALL SAINTS (ORIGINAL)**
This church was located at 25th Place and Wallace. It was established in 1875 and razed in 1973. See All Saints–St. Anthony.

BOTTOM
ST. BARBARA
The architectural offices of Worthman and Steinbach, who designed many of Chicago's Polish Cathedral–style churches, built this octagon-shaped Renaissance church in 1910 at Archer and Throop Streets. Serving the Polish community in Bridgeport, St. Barbara is the patron saint of architects and artillerymen.

Chicago Catholic Churches

ST. AGNES OF BOHEMIA
Originally a Czech parish called Blessed Agnes, the parish was established in 1904. The Renaissance Revival church was built in 1926 at 27th Street and Central Park.

A Sketchbook

TOP **ST. JEROME (CROATIAN)**
This Croatian parish was established in 1912, and they originally worshiped in an old German Lutheran church at 15th and Wentworth. In 1922, the congregation purchased a Swedish Lutheran church in Armour Square at 29th Street and Princeton. The church was heavily renovated, including a new façade, in 1954.

MIDDLE **ST. BRIDGET**
This Irish parish was established in 1850, founded by (Old) St. Patrick's Church. This Romanesque church was built in 1906 at 2940 South Archer and was the first Catholic church in Bridgeport. Mayor Richard J. Daley married his wife, "Sis," here, but even that history couldn't save the church from being razed in 1992.

BOTTOM **ST. LUCIA**
Originally a mission of Santa Maria Incoronata, this Italian parish was established in 1943 at 3022 South Wells. The parishes were merged in 1953 after the Santa Maria Incoronata Church became St. Therese Chinese.

TOP **ST. JOHN NEPOCEME**
Established in 1871 by Bohemians, the church at 30th and Lowe was built in 1903 and closed in 1990.

BOTTOM **MONASTERY OF THE HOLY CROSS**
Established in 1883, the Immaculate Conception BVM Church was closed in 1979 and used as a warehouse for the archdiocese until 1990, when the Monastery of the Holy Cross order took over the church at 31st Street and Aberdeen.

ST. MARY OF PERPETUAL HELP
Established in 1882 as a mission of St. Adalbert's, this Byzantine-Romanesque church was designed by architect Henry Englebert and built in 1903. The church was consecrated free from debt by Archbishop Quigley, making it the first Polish church in the United States to do so.

Chicago Catholic Churches

TOP **ST. DAVID**
The tiny Irish parish of St. David was established in 1905 at 32nd Street and Emerald. It merged with Bridgeport Catholic Academy in 1985, but in 1996, it was closed and razed.

MIDDLE **ST. GEORGE**
Established in 1892 and known as St. George Lithuanian, this Gothic Revival church stood at 33rd Street and Lituanica. The parish closed in 1990 due to the changing demographics, but before it was razed, all of the church's arts, artifacts and furniture were donated to a new parish formed in the old country of Latvia, which was newly independent from the Soviet Union.

BOTTOM
OUR LADY OF GOOD COUNSEL
The parish was founded in 1901. This two-story brick church and combined school was located at 3532 South Hermitage until it was closed in 2008 after merging with Blessed Sacrament.

A Sketchbook

TOP **ST. MAURICE**
Established in 1890 by Germans as St. Mauritius, this church at 36th Street and Hoyne merged with Blessed Sacrament in 2008 and later closed in 2020.

MIDDLE **ST. MONICA**
Chicago's first African American parish was established in 1889 in the Bronzeville neighborhood near 36th Street and Dearborn. The church closed after merging with St. Elizabeth in 1924.

BOTTOM **NATIVITY OF OUR LORD**
Founded in 1869 and built three years later at 37th and Union, this Romanesque Bridgeport church, designed by architect Patrick Keely, broke ground on the former site of horse stables. As the story goes, since Jesus was born in a stable, they decided to name the parish Nativity.

TOP **SS. PETER AND PAUL**
Established in 1895, the Roman Renaissance church located at 38th and Paulina, in the McKinley Park neighborhood, was built in 1907. It was closed in 2008.

BOTTOM **ST. JOSEPH/ST. ANNE**
French Catholics established St. Joseph Parish in 1889. The church was built in 1891 at 38th Place and California. In 1909, the Shrine of St. Anne was built within, and in 1916, a holy relic—a piece of bone from the body of St. Anne—was gifted to the church. In 1991, the parish merged with St. Agnes and became Our Lady of Fatima-Shrine of St. Anne.

A Sketchbook

TOP **ST. GEORGE**
Established in 1884, this German parish served the Union Stockyard workers near Pershing and Wentworth. Construction for the Dan Ryan Expressway in the 1950s demolished most of its parish, and it consolidated with St. Cecelia's Church in 1969. It was eventually closed and razed.

BOTTOM **ST. AGNES**
Irish immigrants established St. Agnes in 1878. The church at 39th and Washtenaw was built in 1905. The parish merged with Our Lady of Fatima–Shrine of St. Anne in 1991 and was demolished shortly thereafter.

Chicago Catholic Churches

TOP **HOLY ANGELS** Sisters of Mercy established this parish in 1880. This French Romanesque church at 605 East Oakwood Boulevard was built in 1897. The church was designed by architect James J. Egan when the Irish parish was still in its infancy. Today, it is one of the largest African American congregations in the city.

BOTTOM **ST. ELIZABETH** The oldest African American parish in Chicago was established in 1881. The church, located at 41st and Wabash, was home to the United States' first African American priest, Father Tolton. A fire destroyed the original church in 1930, and the church seen today was rebuilt in Modern-style architecture in 1989.

ST. GABRIEL
Burnham and Root designed this Romanesque church at 4501 South Lowe. It is called the church that the stockyards built, in that the pastor at the time, Father Maurice Dorney, was able to convince meatpacking moguls Swift and Armour to pay for the church.

TOP **ST. CECELIA**
This Irish church in the Fuller Park neighborhood was established in 1885, with the church built at 45th and Wells. The parish was consolidated and merged with St. Anne in 1971 to form St. Charles Lwanga. It was eventually razed in 1972.

BOTTOM **IMMACULATE HEART OF MARY VICARIATE**
The parish was originally a mission of Holy Cross when they first worshiped in a butcher shop off 43rd Street. The church at 4515 South Ashland was established as a vicariate in 1943.

HOLY CROSS
Established in 1904, this Baroque, Polish Cathedral–style church, designed by Czech architect Joseph Molitor, was built at 46th and Hermitage in 1913 to minister to the Lithuanian Back of the Yards workers. The parish closed in 1983, but masses continued until 2003.

Perhaps in the struggle to defend religious liberty for our churches and for all Americans, our greatest weapon is neither the voting booth nor the legal brief but the prayers that we and our worshipping communities lift up to Almighty.

—*Francis Cardinal George*

A Sketchbook

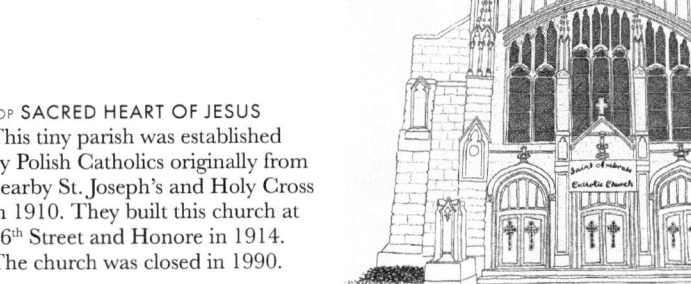

TOP **SACRED HEART OF JESUS**
This tiny parish was established by Polish Catholics originally from nearby St. Joseph's and Holy Cross in 1910. They built this church at 46th Street and Honore in 1914. The church was closed in 1990.

MIDDLE **ST. AMBROSE**
This Irish parish in the Kenwood neighborhood was established in 1904, and this Gothic structure was built in 1926. The church at 47th and Ellis was designed by Zachary Taylor Davis, the same architect as the White Sox's old home, Comiskey Park.

BOTTOM **ST. ROSE OF LIMA**
Established in 1881 by the Irish immigrants working in the Union stockyards, the church was located at 48th and Ashland and was closed and razed in 1990.

Chicago Catholic Churches

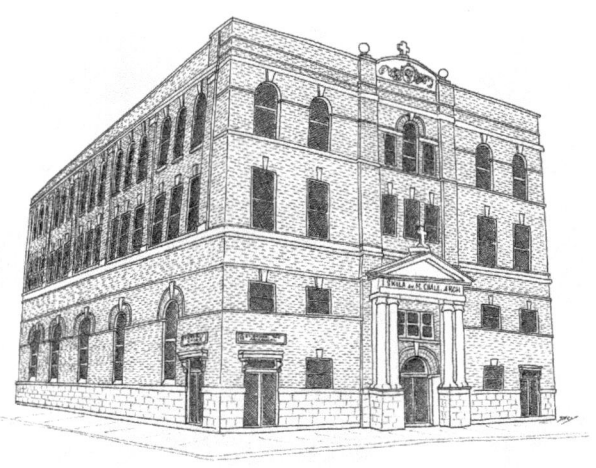

TOP **ST. MICHAEL THE ARCHANGEL**
This Slovak parish established in 1898 was later built as a combined school and church at 48th and Damen. The parish was extinguished in 2020 after merging with St. Joseph.

BOTTOM **ST. JOSEPH (SHRINE OF)**
This Polish parish was established in 1887. The Baroque-style church that stands today was built in 1914. The church was closed in 1990 but made a remarkable comeback as the Shrine of St. Joseph in 1998. In 2020, the archdiocese consolidated several nearby churches, creating one large parish of St. Joseph.

TOP **CORPUS CHRISTI**
A largely Irish congregation built this church at 48th Street and Martin Luther King Jr. Drive in an Italian Renaissance style in 1916. The church's name translates to "body of Christ."

BOTTOM **ST. CYRIL AND METHODIUS**
Prolific architect Joseph Molitor designed this Renaissance church at 5001 South Hermitage. It was built in 1913 for Bohemian Catholics working in the stockyards. Molitor, Bohemian-born himself, designed a number of Chicago churches. The church was closed in 1990 and is currently a Seventh-day Adventist church.

ST. JOHN THE BAPTIST
French settlers established this parish in 1892. The ornate Baroque-style church was closed in 1989 and now serves as the Ebenezer House of Prayer.

TOP **ST. AUGUSTINE**
Established in 1879, this Gothic church used to tower over the corner of 51st and Laflin. The parish had a grammar school, a high school and its own bowling alley. The church was closed and razed in 1990.

BOTTOM **ST. BASIL**
With a footprint in the shape of a cross, this Byzantine church was built in 1926 by architect Joe W. McCarthy. After the German and Irish parishioners moved, the church merged, was renamed for a time and finally razed in 1998.

Chicago Catholic Churches

TOP **ST. ANNE**
The Irish parishioners established St. Anne's Parish in 1865 and for a time worshiped in an old Jewish synagogue. In 1869, this Gothic church was built at Garfield and Wentworth. The construction of the Dan Ryan Expressway changed the neighborhood as well as its demographics. St. Anne consolidated with other nearby parishes to become St. Charles Lwanga before closing for good in 1990.

BOTTOM **ST. CHARLES LWANGA**
This African American church was established in 1971 after the closing and merging of several parishes, including St. George, St. Anne and St. Cecelia. The parish was closed and razed in 1990.

VISITATION
On the Feast Day of Mary's Visitation in 1886, this Irish parish was established. This Medieval Gothic church was built in 1899 at Garfield Boulevard and Peoria. The parish merged with St. Basil in 1990.

ST. JOHN OF GOD
Established in 1909 and built in 1920 at 1234 West 52nd Street, this Henry J. Schlacks Renaissance Revival loomed large over Ogden Park until it was closed in 1992. Before this iconic church was demolished, however, the façade was saved and rebuilt as St. Raphael's Church in upstate Old Mill Creek, Illinois.

ST. RAPHAEL
Established as an Irish parish in 1901, this church and school combined structure stood at 60th and Justine until it closed in 1989. The building is used today as the Boulevard Community Arts and Theatre Center.

ST. MARTIN
The parish, established in 1894, was named for St. Martin of Tours, the German soldier and saint. The German Gothic church was built in 1895 at 59th and Princeton. As the demographics changed, the church was renamed for St. Martin De Porres, the Black Dominican brother of Lima, Peru. It was closed in 1989.

TOP **ST. THOMAS THE APOSTLE**
This church, recognized as the first Modern architecture church in the United States, was created by architect Francis Barry Byrne, former student of Frank Lloyd Wright, at 5476 South Kimbark in 1924. The parish was established by Hyde Park Irish Catholics in 1868.

BOTTOM **ASSUMPTION BVM**
Croatian Catholics from St. Cecelia founded this parish in 1901. By the time this Mid-Century Modern church was built, the congregation was predominantly Polish. The church closed in 1990 and is now home to the United Faith Temple.

A Sketchbook

TOP **ST. ANSELM**
This Washington Park parish was established by Irish Catholics in 1909. In 1925, Irish-born architect Charles Wallace designed this Romanesque church on 61st Street, making it the first Catholic church built on Michigan Boulevard.

BOTTOM **ST. THEODORE**
Named for the first pastor's aunt, Sister Theodore, this Irish parish established in 1916 served the Irish Catholics in the combined school and church at 62nd and Paulina. The parish was closed in 1976 and eventually razed.

Chicago Catholic Churches

TOP **OUR LADY OF SOLACE**
Established by Irish Catholics in 1916 at 62nd and Sangamon, this Renaissance Revival church was closed after the parish merged with St. Martin in 1988.

BOTTOM **ST. RITA OF CASCIA**
The first Augustine parish in Chicago was established in 1905. This Renaissance/Romanesque church at 63rd and Fairfield was designed by architect Arthur F. Moratz and completed in 1950.

A Sketchbook

TOP **ST. CLARA–ST. GELASIUS**
The long history of this Italian Renaissance church, built in 1927 at 64th and Woodlawn, includes becoming a national Shrine of the Little Flower in 1925. The church was renamed St. Clara/ St. Cyril after a merge and then renamed after the African St. Gelasius after nearly losing the entire church to arson. The parish closed in 2002 and was scheduled to be demolished until it received last-minute landmark status in 2004. The church is currently the shrine of Christ the King Church.

BOTTOM **ST. BERNARD**
Established by Irish Catholics in 1887, the very first masses for this parish were held in Maloney's beer hall until the combined church and school were built at 65th and Harvard. The roof collapsed in a snowstorm in 1967, and the structure was eventually razed.

Chicago Catholic Churches

TOP **HOLY CROSS**
This Irish parish began in a grocery store on Cottage Grove before building this Renaissance Revival church at 65th and Maryland. The parish was closed in 1990 after merging with St. Cyril and St. Gelasius, and it is now called the Light of the World Church.

BOTTOM **ST. BENEDICT THE AFRICAN**
After the mass closing and merging of several Englewood parishes, this parish was established and built in 1989 on the grounds of the razed St. Bernard's at 71st and Honore. The church, built in an Ultra-Modernist style, boasts the largest baptismal font in the United States.

ST. BRENDAN
In a neighborhood originally nicknamed the "Cabbage Patch," St. Brendan's Parish was formed by the Irish Catholics in 1899. A few years later, this Gothic church was built at 67th and Racine. The parish closed in 1988 after a mass merge with St. Benedict the African and was razed in 1989.

Chicago Catholic Churches

TOP **ST. JUSTIN MARTYR** Founded in 1916 by Irish Catholics in Englewood, the church, designed by noted architect Joe W. McCarthy, was built the very next year. Although they closed in 1989, the church and school grounds remain part of the archdiocese.

BOTTOM **ST. COLUMBANUS** In 1909, this parish was established in the Park Manor neighborhood. In 1923, this Gothic church was built to serve the largely Irish population, but as demographics changed, so did the church, making it one of the oldest African American Catholic churches in the city.

TOP **ST. PHILIP NERI**
This Tudor Gothic church, designed by Joe W. McCarthy, located at 72nd and Merrill was built in 1928, when much of the South Shore neighborhood was still sand dunes and tree nurseries.

BOTTOM
ST. LAURENCE
The neighborhood was called Parkside when this parish was established in 1883. This Gothic church at 72nd Street and Dorchester was built in 1911 and closed in 2002. Despite efforts to preserve the structure, the church was razed in 2014.

Chicago Catholic Churches

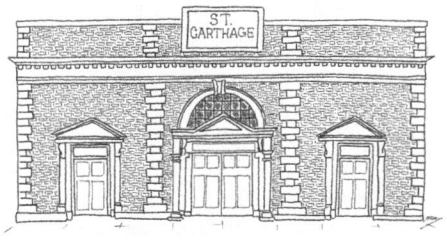

TOP **ST. CARTHAGE**
This simple brick one-story church was built in 1921 at 73rd and Yale. The parish was closed in 1989 and merged with St. Benedict the African East.

MIDDLE **ST. BRIDE**
This South Shore parish was established in 1893 by Irish Catholics from St. Kevin's. The French Gothic church was built in 1909 at 78th Street and Coles and closed in 2020.

BOTTOM **ST. LEO THE GREAT**
Once the largest parish in the city, St. Leo the Great, established in 1885, served Irish Catholics in a large part of the South Side until being divided up by St. Kilian and St. Sabina. The Renaissance church at 78th and Emerald Avenue was closed in 2002, and the grounds were used to build a home for veterans. The church was razed; however, the original bell tower still stands.

A Sketchbook

TOP **ST. FRANCIS DEPAULA**
Established in 1911 by Italian Catholics, this Romanesque limestone church stood overlooking Grand Crossing Park at 78th and Dobson. The parish was closed in 1991 and is now the New Life Covenant Church.

MIDDLE **ST. DOROTHY**
This tiny church at 78th and Vernon, established in 1916, was intended to be a much larger structure until the nation went into a depression and the parish was forced to keep the church one story tall. Still an impressive Gothic Revival structure, the church was home to the archdiocese's first ordained African American priest, Father Rollins Lambert.

BOTTOM **ST. SABINA**
Joe W. McCarthy built this English Gothic church at 7821 South Throop Street in 1933. The parish has remained strong in the Auburn Highlands neighborhood and has the distinction of hosting Chicago's very first St. Patrick's Day parade.

OUR LADY OF PEACE
This territorial parish was established in 1919. The church, at 79th and Jeffery, was designed by Joseph W. McCarthy in 1935. The structure is Roman influenced with hints of Art Deco. Today, the church is one of very few in the United States that hosts French Haitian masses.

TOP **ST. THERESE OF THE INFANT JESUS**
Established in 1925 and known to the parishioners simply as "Little Flower," this Gothic church at 80th and Wood Street once served a large Irish Catholic congregation. Closed in 1993, the church is now home to the Greater Mount Hebron Baptist Church.

BOTTOM **ST. BRONISLAVA**
This parish was established in 1928, while the services were held in the basement of Bowen High School. The church and combined school was built a short time later at 87th and Colfax but closed in 2014. It remains in use today by the Word of Life Ministries.

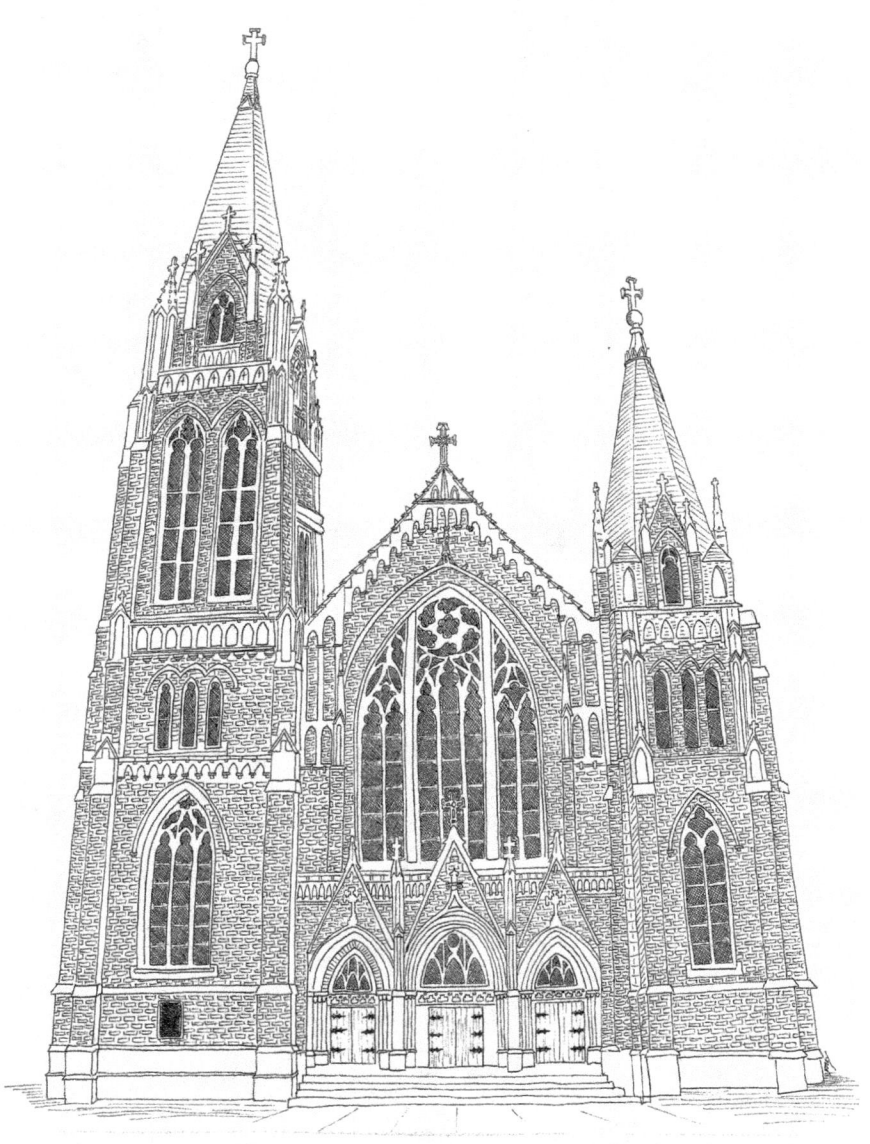

ST. MICHAEL
This parish was established by Polish steel mill workers in a neighborhood known as "The Bush." In 1909, architect William J. Brinkman designed this iconic Gothic church at 83rd and South Shore Drive in the style of the old-country Polish cathedrals. The parish was also home to Bishop Paul Rhode, the first Polish-born bishop in the United States.

TOP **ST. MARY MAGDALENE**
This parish was formed in 1910 to address overcrowding of the Polish Catholics from the nearby Immaculate Conception Parish. The simple Romanesque church was built in 1954 at 84th and Marquette and closed in 2015.

MIDDLE **ST. FELICITAS**
Established in 1919, this Romanesque church was designed by architect George S. Smith. Built in 1920 at 84th and Blackstone in the Avalon Park neighborhood, the parish lasted nearly one century but was closed in 2019.

BOTTOM **ST. CLOTILDE**
Named for the patron saint of queens, St. Clotilde Parish, established in 1928, began as a territorial parish worshiping in Mercy High School. This small Gothic church, designed by architect Charles L. Wallace, was built in 1930 at 84th Street and Calumet.

Chicago Catholic Churches

TOP **ST. KILIAN**
This parish was founded in 1905 by the Irish and German parishioners who lived west of St. Leo the Great. The Romanesque church, designed by architect Joseph W. McCarthy, was built a year later at 87th Street and May.

MIDDLE **ST. JOHN BAPTIST**
This tiny house church located on Burley just south of 91st Street was established in 1909 after moving into what was once an old Protestant church. The church closed in 1993.

BOTTOM **ST. JOSEPH**
This tiny Lithuanian parish was established in 1900, and the small single-story church, on 88th between Marqeutte and Saginaw, has been closed since 1987. The building is now used by the McKinley public school.

A Sketchbook

IMMACULATE CONCEPTION
This grand Renaissance Revival church at 88th Street and Commercial was built in 1899, designed by architect Martin Carr, influenced by the Polish cathedral style. The parish was closed in 1982 and later reopened under Daughters of Mary Immaculate of Guadalupe.

ST. ETHELREDA
Named after the Irish Roman Catholic church in Ely, England, the parish was established in 1926. The church was built in a modern Romanesque style in 1953 but closed in 2007.

ST. AILBE
Also known as St. Katharine of Drexel, this small Modern church at 91st and Harper was originally an Irish parish and named after a church in Tipperary, Ireland.

A Sketchbook

TOP **ST. JOACHIM**
Originally founded as a mission of nearby St. Ailbe in 1894, this Neo-Gothic church, built in 1896, was designed by architect George S. Smith. The church, located at 91st Street and Langley, closed in 2019 and is slated for demolition.

BOTTOM
SS. PETER AND PAUL
Before being annexed into the city of Chicago, this German Catholic parish was established in 1882 when the neighborhood was part of the town of Colehour. Located at the corner of 91st and Exchange, the church closed in 1986.

Chicago Catholic Churches

OUR LADY OF GUADALUPE
Chicago's first Mexican parish was established in 1924 at 91st and Brandon. The church was built in a Spanish Mission style and ministered to local steelworkers. In 1929, the church became a National Shrine of St. Jude.

OUR LADY OF HUNGARY
As it's named, Hungarian Catholics established this parish in 1934 at 93rd and Kimbark in the Burnside neighborhood. The church was closed in 1987 and eventually razed, and the grounds are now part of the St. Ailbe senior homes.

A Sketchbook

TOP **ST. PATRICK**
East Side Irish Catholics established this parish in 1857 as a mission of St. James. The combined church and school stood near 95th and Commercial until it was closed in 1986. The founding of this St. Patrick is why the "other" church is referred to as "Old St. Pat's."

MIDDLE **ST. GEORGE**
Slovenian Catholics established this parish in 1903, and the Romanesque church at 96th and Ewing was built a year later. The church closed in 2020 after merging with Annunciata, St. Frances de Sales and St. Kevin.

BOTTOM **SACRED HEART**
Croatians from St. Jerome moved to the South Deering neighborhood and established this parish in 1913. This modern Neo-Gothic church was built in 1964 at 96th and Escanaba.

Chicago Catholic Churches

TOP **OUR LADY GATE OF HEAVEN** African American Catholics established and built this church in 1947. The Modernist church and school is located at 99th and Cranston in the once predominantly Jewish neighborhood of Jeffery Manor. A map view shows that the streets were designed to represent a menorah.

MIDDLE **ST. THADDEUS** Founded as a mission of Holy Name of Mary, this parish was established in 1962 and built shortly thereafter. The simple frame church is located at 9550 South Harvard.

BOTTOM **ST. HELENA OF THE CROSS** Established in 1946, this small church and school was located at 10115 South Parnell. The church was closed in 2014 and now serves as the South Side campus of Victory Cathedral.

A Sketchbook

TOP
ST. JOHN DE LA SALLE
This territorial parish was established in 1948. The brick church with the attached grammar school is located at 102nd and Vernon in the Rosemoor neighborhood.

MIDDLE **ST. KEVIN**
The parishioners celebrated mass in Ambrose Gagne's Hall at 106th and Torrence until their church was built up the block in 1886. The red brick rectangle combined church and school is located at 105th and Torrence. The church was slated to close in 2020, but parishioners successfully petitioned for the church to remain open for services.

BOTTOM
ST. FRANCIS DE SALES
German Catholics established this parish in 1889 as a mission of Ss. Peter and Paul at 91st and Exchange. The brick Gothic-influenced church stands at 102nd Street and Avenue J, across the street from the high school of the same name. The church was closed in 2020 after consolidating with Annunciata.

Chicago Catholic Churches

TOP **HOLY ROSARY**
Established in 1907 by Slovenian Catholics, the church at the corner of 108th and Perry was built in 1910. The church was closed in 1973 and is now the home of the Kingdom of Christ Baptist Church.

MIDDLE **ALL SAINTS**
Designed by Lithuanian architect S. Kudokus, this Neo-Gothic Modernist structure was built in 1906 with its unusual open bell tower at 108th and State Streets. The parish closed in 1989.

BOTTOM **ANNUNCIATA**
This Modernist church was built in 1941 at 11131 South Avenue H. The parishioners originally worshiped in a nearby garage while the church was under construction. In 2020, the church merged with St. George, St. Kevin and St. Francis De Sales, with Annunciata being the home church.

A Sketchbook

TOP **HOLY NAME OF MARY**
This modern church, established by African American Catholics in 1940, is located at 112th and Loomis in the Morgan Park neighborhood.

MIDDLE **ST. WILLIBRORD**
The only Dutch Roman Catholic church in Chicago was established in 1900. Located at 114th and Edgebrook, the church was renamed after taking over the former St. Louis de France Catholic Church. The church closed in 1988.

BOTTOM **SACRED HEART (MISSION OF HOLY NAME OF MARY)**
This tiny church at 11652 South Church Street was built in 1904 to serve French Canadian laborers from the nearby Purington Brickyards. The entire church is built from Purington bricks. The church survived the archdiocese's attempts to shut it down in the late 1970s and has recently been fully renovated.

HOLY ROSARY
This church was established by Irish Catholics in 1882 when the territory was still the town of Pullman. George Pullman himself was to finance the construction of the church until a falling-out with the pastor, who called him a "capitalistic Czar." Located at 113th Street and Martin Luther King Jr. Drive, the Gothic church was once frequented by a young future president, Barack Obama, who worked in an office in the church as a community organizer. The church was closed in 2011 and is now home to the Greater Tabernacle Cathedral.

Anyone who's driven along the Kennedy has seen the silhouettes of steeples jabbing at the sky—steeples as diverse as the houses of worship that they belong to, and the immigrants that built them, and the communities who call those neighborhoods home to this day.

—*President Barack Obama in his speech
at the Copernicus Center in Chicago*

Chicago Catholic Churches

TOP **ST. ANTHONY**
The Italian parish of St. Anthony of Padua was established in 1903. The Modern Neo-Gothic church at Indiana and Kensington Streets was built in 1961 in the Roseland neighborhood.

BOTTOM
ST. LOUIS DE FRANCE
French settlers established this parish in 1886 at 117th and State, which at one point was called St. Ambrose. The church closed in 1973 when it merged with All Saints Parish. Today, the church is home to Bethesda Apostolic Faith Church.

ST. SALOMEA
The pastor of St. Columba in Hegewisch was tired of traveling so far to hold mass, so legend has it, he founded this parish in 1898 for the Polish Catholics in Roseland. The Gothic church at 118th and Indiana was built in 1900 and closed in 1990. It served as a Baptist church before eventually being demolished.

Chicago churches often do a remarkable job representing this heavenly feast [of St. Catherine of Genoa]*, providing an anticipatory experience of a glorified future and making Chicago a more heavenly city itself. The beauty of heaven draws people in, inspires them to ask questions and learn and they emerge transformed to in turn transform the earthly city. Such is the power of beauty, truth and goodness in well-designed and ornamented liturgical architecture. Today's church architects would do well to learn the lessons these churches continue to teach.*

—*Denis McNamara*, Heavenly City

A Sketchbook

TOP **ST. CATHERINE OF GENOA**
This Greek Revival church with a school attached is located at 118th and Lowe. Established in 1893, the building went through many changes, including the new Modernist façade in the 1950s. The church closed in 1990 when it merged with Maternity BVM. Today, the church and campus are home to St. James Ministries.

MIDDLE **ASSUMPTION BVM (CLOSED)**
This parish was established in 1903 by Polish Catholics, with the church at 123rd Street and Parnell being built a year later. The parish closed after merging with St. Catherine of Genoa. The church is now home to a community Christian Family Center.

BOTTOM
SS. PETER AND PAUL
The last Lithuanian Chicago Catholic church still in use was established in 1914. The current Modernist Gothic church was built in 1959 at 125th Street and Halsted.

Chicago Catholic Churches

TOP **ST. FLORIAN**
Named for the patron saint of firemen, this parish, established in 1903, sits in the heart of the Hegewisch neighborhood. The combined church and school is located at 131st and Houston.

MIDDLE **ST. NICHOLAS**
Architect William J. Brinkman designed this Neo-Gothic church built in 1896. Built for the German Catholics in Roseland, the church closed in 1973, and after serving several years as various Baptist churches, it was finally demolished in 2019.

BOTTOM
OUR LADY OF THE GARDENS
Located in the Altgeld Public Housing Complex, this Romanesque Modern church at 133rd and Langley was built in 1952. The parish was originally a mission of St. Mary of the Assumption and was known as Our Lady of the Miraculous Medal.

TOP **ST. COLUMBA**
Near the southern tip of Hegewisch, at the corner of 134th and Green Bay, rests this Modernist, one-story brick church. The parish was founded in 1884 as a mission of St. Kevin and closed in 2019.

MIDDLE **ST. MARY OF THE ASSUMPTION**
The southernmost church in the city of Chicago, this parish, located at 138th and Leyden, was established in 1886. The church and school campus, bordering the suburbs of Dalton and Riverdale, was closed in 2011.

BOTTOM **ST. WALTER**
The architectural firm of Gaul and Voosen called this Mid-Century church an example of International Modernism. Established in 1953 and completed in 1956, the combined church and school is located at 118th and Western.

Chicago Catholic Churches

TOP **ST. CAJETAN**
Morgan Park's second Roman Catholic church is this English Gothic Revival built in 1943. The parish was established in 1927 by Irish Catholics who branched off from the French Sacred Heart, and the masses were held in a wood-frame church until architect Gerald Berry designed this structure at 112th and Artesian.

MIDDLE **ST. CHRISTINA**
As the population of Mount Greenwood grew, so did this parish, established in 1926. After the parishioners worshiped in temporary quarters and later in a simple brick structure, this modern Romanesque church at 111th and Christiana was completed in 1956. They held their inaugural mass on Christmas Day.

BOTTOM
ST. JOHN FISHER
Located at 103rd and Fairfield, this parish, established in 1948, built this Mid-Century Modernist church in 1956. Over the years, there have been dramatic modifications, but the sleek modern look has never been compromised.

A Sketchbook

TOP **ST. BARNABAS**
This parish, established in 1917, once stretched from the neighborhood of Fernwood to suburban Palos Heights. This New Formalist church at 101st Street and Longwood was designed by architect Carl E. Hundreiser and completed in 1969.

BOTTOM **ST. MARGARET OF SCOTLAND**
In what was once the town of Washington Heights, this parish was formed in 1874. Many consider it to be the mother church of the South Side, in that several new parishes were formed within its original boundaries. The current Gothic church at 99th and Throop was built in 1926.

Chicago Catholic Churches

TOP **CHRIST THE KING**
This Beverly parish was established in 1936. In 1955, Fox and Fox architects built this Mid-Century Modern church at 93rd and Hamilton.

MIDDLE **ST. THOMAS MORE**
This parish was established in 1947, and this Ultra-Modernist church was designed by Barry and Kay architectural firm. The oval on the rectangular church at 81st and California was completed in 1958. It was the first new church in the city of Chicago post–World War II.

BOTTOM
ST. BEDE THE VENERABLE
An airplane hangar in the old Ashburn airport was the home for this parish's first masses in the early 1950s. This early Modernist church at 83rd Street and Kostner was built in 1961.

A Sketchbook

TOP **ST. DENIS**
The neighborhood of Ashburn was literally named for the ash piles in the area from locomotives and downtown industry. This parish was established in 1951, and this Modern church at 83rd Street and St. Louis was built shortly thereafter.

MIDDLE
QUEEN OF THE UNIVERSE
This practical combined school and church was established in 1955 and built a short time later. Located at 71st Street and Hamlin, the church is a fine example of Mid-Century Modern architecture. The parish closed in 2021 after a merge with St. Adrian and became the new Mary, Mother of Mercy Parish.

BOTTOM **ST. ADRIAN**
Named for the patron saint of soldiers, this parish was established in 1928 before it had any official territory. Legend has it that Father Leo MacNamara held mass from the trunk of his Hudson sedan before this Tudor Gothic church was built at 70th and Washtenaw. The parish closed after a merge with Queen of the Universe to become the new parish of Mary, Mother of Mercy.

TOP **NATIVITY BVM** The growing Lithuanian Catholic population built this grand church at 69th and Washtenaw. While the parish was established in 1927, the church wasn't built until 1957 by architect Jonas Mulokas, in a Baroque style heavily influenced by Lithuanian folk design.

BOTTOM **ST. MARY OF MOUNT CARMEL** Italian Catholics founded this West Englewood parish in 1892. This Romanesque church at Marquette and Hermitage was closed in 1976 and is now home to the St. Andrew's Temple Baptist Church.

A Sketchbook

TOP **ST. MARY STAR OF THE SEA**
An overflow of parishioners from St. Nicholas Tolentine established this parish in 1948. This flat Mid-Century Modern church with school attached was built in 1955 and is located at 64th Street and Kilbourn.

MIDDLE
ST. RENE GOUPIL
This dark red Postmodern church stands at 6340 South New England. The parish was formed in 1959 as the neighborhood of West Clearing and Nottingham Park continued to grow. The parish was closed in 2020 after a merge with St. Symphorosa to create the new parish of Two Holy Martyrs.

BOTTOM
ST. SYMPHOROSA AND HER SEVEN SONS
Known simply as St. Syms by the parishioners, this parish was established in 1927 with its first masses held in the Clearing Town Hall. The Romanesque church stands at 62nd and Austin, but the parish was closed after it merged with St. Rene's to become the new parish of Two Holy Martyrs in 2020.

Chicago Catholic Churches

TOP **ST. NICHOLAS OF TOLENTINE**
Founded as an Augustinian mission in 1909, the parish was established in 1916. This Tudor Gothic church at 62nd and Lawndale was built in 1939.

MIDDLE **ST. TIRIBIUS**
Established in 1927, this parish was founded by Polish Catholics when most of the area was still prairie. A church was built in the 1930s but was turned into classrooms after this Modern Romanesque structure was built in 1952 at 57th Street and Karlov.

BOTTOM **ST. GALL**
The town of Eldson was home to this brand-new parish in the late 1800s before being annexed into the city of Chicago. After several structures and moving several times, this Mid-Century Modern church at 55th and Kedzie was built in 1958 with the novel idea that "the altar should be the true center of the church," according to Monsignor Hishen.

ST. CLARE MONTEFALCO
In 1928, this parish was founded as a mission of St. Rita. This Romanesque church at 55th Street and Washtenaw was built in 1954. The parish closed after a merge and once again became a mission of St. Rita in 2020.

ST. CAMILLUS
Originally called St. Florian and established in 1918 as a mission of St. Joseph's from the Argo/Summit neighborhood, the parish was formed to serve the growing neighborhoods of Garfield Ridge and Sleepy Hollow. The parish was named St. Camillus in order to distinguish itself from the already named Hegewisch parish in 1921. This Modern Romanesque church was built in 1958 but closed in 2020 after merging with St. Jane de Chantel.

ST. DANIEL THE PROPHET
Better known simply as St. Dan's by parishioners, this parish was established in the Garfield Ridge neighborhood in 1947. The Romanesque church at 54th Street and Nashville was built shortly thereafter.

ST. JANE DE CHANTEL
Established in 1954, the parish built this Ultra-Modernist church in 1964. The design is an example of form follows function architecture by William P. Pavlecic. The parish merged with St. Camillus and is now called St. Faustina Kowalska.

ST. SIMON THE APOSTLE
This grand brick combined church and school at 52nd and California was built by Slovak Catholics. Established in 1926, construction began soon after. The church holds the distinction of holding the last Slovenian-language mass in the city.

ST. RICHARD
Named after Bishop Richard Wyche of Chichester, England, this parish was established in 1928. The church was once located within the school building until a new brick structure was built in 1959 at 50th Street and Kostner.

Chicago Catholic Churches

ST. BRUNO
"The Florist Shop" was the nickname for the very first church built by Polish laymen after establishing this parish in 1925, due to the frame structure and glass ceiling windows. In 1956, this Romanesque church was built at 48th Street and Harding.

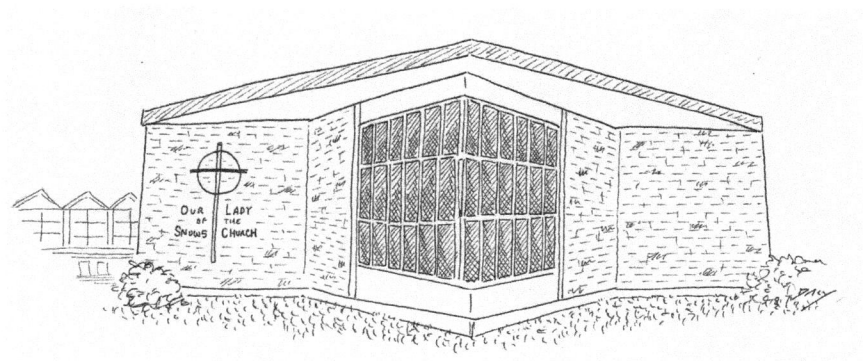

OUR LADY OF SNOWS
Legend has it that this parish was established after a terrible rainstorm and flood struck the Archer Heights and Vittum Park neighborhood in 1959. This Ultra-Modernist church and school combined was completed in 1961 at 48th Street and Leamington.

A Sketchbook

IMMACULATE CONCEPTION
This Brighton Park Lithuanian parish was established in 1914. The Mid-Century Modernist church was later built at 44th Street and California, holding its very first mass on Christmas Day 1964.

ST. PANCRATIUS
With the congregation originally worshiping in Five Holy Martyrs Church, St. Pancratius became a parish in 1924, and members worshiped in a church near 41st Street and Sacramento. In 1959, the new modern Romanesque church was built at 40th and Sacramento.

TOP
FIVE HOLY MARTYRS Pope John Paul II said mass here during a visit in 1979. The parish was established in 1908. The Spanish Mission–style church at 43rd and Richmond was built in 1920 with major exterior work and modern changes in 1963. The parish merged with several other churches in 1999, and the school was later named after the visiting pope.

BOTTOM
HOLY INNOCENTS The architectural firm of Worthman and Steinbach designed this Spanish Romanesque church with Byzantine influences and inspired by the Polish Cathedral style. Located at 735 North Armour, the parish was established in 1905 and the church built in 1912. The church survived a massive fire in 1962, and the entire interior was rebuilt and redesigned, with the finishing touches completed in 2005.

A Sketchbook

TOP **HOLY GUARDIAN ANGEL**
Father Paolo Ponsilione, a Jesuit teacher at St. Ignatius, formed this parish in 1899 for the Italian Catholics who lived too far from Assumption Church to attend mass. Located at 860 West Cabrini, the church was built within the year, and this practical combined school and church was completed in the 1950s. However, the church sat in the path of the new Dan Ryan Expressway and was razed shortly thereafter. The parish officially dissolved in 1960.

MIDDLE **OUR LADY OF GOOD COUNSEL**
This tiny church at Walton and Western Avenue was established by Bohemians in 1889. The church did not survive the century, as it was closed in 1989 and turned into condominiums.

BOTTOM **ST. STEPHEN KING OF HUNGARY**
Established in 1934 by Hungarian Catholics originally as St. Emeric, the parish changed its name when this church was built in 1938 at 2015 West Augusta.

HOLY FAMILY
Recognized as the first Jesuit parish in Chicago, this impressive Gothic church at Roosevelt and May was built in 1860. Legend has it that during the Chicago Fire, Father Damen prayed in the steeple window that the church be spared. After surviving unscathed, the parish began a tradition of keeping seven candles lit in the Shrine of Our Lady of Perpetual Help, a practice that continues to this day.

A Sketchbook

ST. JOHN CANTIUS
In a neighborhood once known as the "Polish Patch," this parish, established in 1893, built this grand Renaissance-Baroque church at 821 North Carpenter in 1898. Architect Alphonsus Druiding designed this church, and the parishioners nicknamed it the "Golden Church" due to the amount of gold in its interior design.

In Chicago our God lurks everywhere. In the elevated train's husky roar. Beside the blinking lights of intensive care. In the clamor of the soybean trading floor, with those who suffer poverty and fright. In the humid mists of the summer by the lake. On the Ryan through an icy night with a young widow weeping at a wake.

—Father Andrew Greeley

ST. MARY OF THE ANGELS
Surrounded by thirty-two nine-foot-tall guardian angel statues along its roofline, this Renaissance church stands at 1850 North Hermitage. The parish was established by Polish Catholics in 1899. Construction of the church was delayed due to World War I and finally completed in 1920.

TOP **ST. STEPHEN**
Known as "Old St. Stephen," this Irish parish was established in 1869. The church sat in the path of the new Kennedy Expressway and was closed and razed in 1950.

BOTTOM **ST. MATTHEW**
The parish was established in 1892, and this Renaissance church stood at the corner of Walnut and Albany until it was closed and razed in 1974.

OUR LADY OF SORROWS BASILICA
In 1956, Pope Pius XII granted this Italian Renaissance church the title of basilica, the first in Illinois. The Servants of Mary (Servites) purchased farmland after establishing this parish in 1874, and the church, located at 3131 West Jackson, was completed in 1902.

TOP **ST. JARLATH**
Originally named St. Aloysius, the parish was established in 1869 by Irish Catholics. This Gothic church at 1713 West Jackson was closed and razed in 1969.

BOTTOM
OUR LADY OF POMPEII
In order to address overcrowding at Holy Guardian Angel, this parish was established in 1910. This church, at Lexington and Lytle, was built in 1923 and became a shrine in 1994.

A Sketchbook

TOP **PRESENTATION**
This West Side parish was established in 1898 by Irish Catholics. This Spanish Romanesque church was located at the corner of Springfield and Polk Streets until it was closed in 1981 and eventually demolished.

BOTTOM
OUR LADY OF ANGELS
Founded in 1894, the parish built this church in 1940. Most Chicagoans know the story of the horrible fire that took the lives of ninety-two children and three nuns. What many people don't realize is that from the tragedy rose new rules and regulations for fire safety. If you've ever had a fire drill in grammar school, the Our Lady of Angels fire is the reason.

Chicago Catholic Churches

TOP **HOLY ROSARY** Italian Catholics west of St. Maria Addolorata established this parish in 1904. This Renaissance church at 614 North Western Avenue was built shortly after the parish formed.

BOTTOM **OUR LADY HELP OF CHRISTIANS** This far West Side church was established by Irish Catholics in 1901. This Renaissance church at Iowa and Leclaire was built shortly thereafter and officially closed in 2005.

A Sketchbook

TOP **OUR LADY OF LOURDES**
Established by Czechs in 1892, this church at 15th and Keeler was closed in 2005 and is now home to Pentecostal Church of Holiness.

MIDDLE **ST. FRANCIS ASSISI**
On the very edge of University of Illinois Chicago's campus, at 813 West Roosevelt, rests this small Gothic church. This formerly German parish on the West Side was established in 1852. The masses are now practiced in the Spanish language.

BOTTOM **SANTA MARIA ADDOLORATA**
The Scalabrinian order established this parish for Italian immigrants in 1903. The original church was destroyed in a fire in 1931. The parish worshiped in an old Swedish Lutheran church until the construction of the Kennedy Expressway forced demolition. Finally, this Mid-Century Modernist church was built in 1960 at Ohio and Ada.

Chicago Catholic Churches

TOP **ST. FINBARR**
Irish Catholics founded this parish in 1900. The combined church and school at 14th and Harding was closed in 1969 and razed shortly thereafter.

MIDDLE AND BOTTOM
HOLY TRINITY
This Italian parish was established in 1885, and shortly thereafter, this small brick church was built. In the late 1950s, the parish razed the original church and built a Modern brick structure at Taylor Street and Wolcott. The church was known as Holy Trinity Medical Center until it was closed in 1990 and is now home to a community medical center.

ST. MALACHY
A small wooden church on the West Side was where this parish was founded in 1882 by Irish Catholics. A larger stone church was built along Western Avenue until it was razed to widen the street. The current church, built in 1929 at Washington and Oakley, was designed by architect Edward T.P. Graham. In 2012, the parish merged with Precious Blood.

Chicago Catholic Churches

TOP **SACRED HEART** This parish was established by Slovaks after dedicating the former Bethlehem Norwegian United Church at Huron and Racine in 1911. Italian Catholics moved the church after it was demolished in 1968 to the corner of Huron and Oakley. The church was closed in 1990.

BOTTOM
PRECIOUS BLOOD This combined church and school at Congress and Western Avenue was closed in 2012 after merging with St. Malachy. The parish served Italian and Irish Catholics and was established in 1907. The structure is now home to an Ombudsman school.

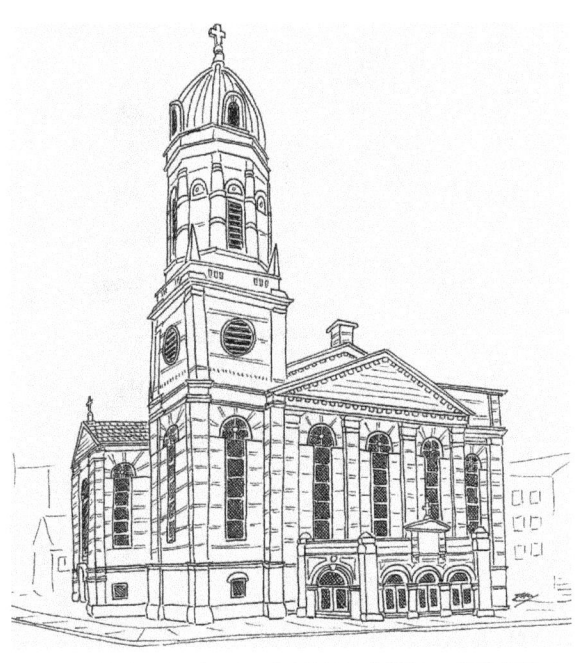

TOP **ST. COLUMBKILLE**
Originally an Irish parish established in 1859, it began as a mission of Old St. Patrick's. This Gothic church once stood at Grand Avenue and Paulina until it was closed and razed in 1975.

BOTTOM
ST. FRANCES XAVIER CABRINI
Pleasant Grove Methodist Baptist Church at Lexington and Sacramento was once St. Frances Xavier Cabrini Catholic Church, also known as Blessed Mother Cabrini, built in 1940. The parish was dissolved in 1987.

Chicago Catholic Churches

TOP **RESURRECTION**
Once a thriving West Side Irish parish, Resurrection was established in 1909, and this Romanesque church closed and razed in 1988.

MIDDLE
ST. CYRIL AND METHODIUS
This combined church and school at Walton and Kildare was built in 1925 and closed in 1987. The structure is now home to Kingsword International Church.

BOTTOM **ST. FRANCIS ASSISI**
German farmers founded this parish in 1909. This Modern Romanesque church was built at Augusta and Kostner and merged with Our Lady of Angels in 1990. In 2021, it became part of the San Jose Luis Sanchez del Rio Parish.

ST. THOMAS AQUINAS
Karl Vitzhum, the architect of this Tudor Gothic church at 5120 West Washington, was also a parishioner. Built in 1923, the twelve-story bell tower remains the tallest structure in the Austin neighborhood. In 1989, the parish was renamed St. Martin de Porres.

ST. ANGELA
This parish, established in 1916, held its first mass in Rockne Movie Theatre on Division Street. This Gothic church at Potomac and Massasoit was built in 1952, closed in 2005 and finally demolished in 2017.

TOP **ST. LUCY**
Established in 1911 when the area was still the town of Austin, this combined church and school at Lake Street and Mayfield was closed in 1977 and is now the home of the Mars Hill Baptist Church.

MIDDLE **ST. PETER CANISIUS**
The parish was established in 1925, and the church was built in 1935. This Romanesque church at North Avenue and Leclaire closed in 2007, but much of the church's interior—including pews, stained-glass windows and altar—was donated to St. Raphael in Old Mill Creek.

BOTTOM **HOLY GHOST**
This parish was established in 1896. The combined church and school at 4341 West Adams closed in 1941 and was razed shortly thereafter.

ST. MEL

Once the largest Irish American parish in the country, this Romanesque church at 4301 West Washington was built shortly after it was founded in 1911. For decades, every Sunday the church would hold six masses in the upper church, six in the lower chapel and six in the nearby Holy Ghost Chapel. The parish merged with Holy Ghost in 1941 and closed in 1988.

A Sketchbook

ST. AGATHA
Irish Catholics in the predominantly Jewish neighborhood along Douglas Boulevard established this parish in 1893. In 1906, this French Romanesque and Byzantine church was built at 3151 West Douglas with an inscription in Latin over the front doors that translated to "The door is open to everyone." True to its motto, the parish now serves a predominantly African American population, and a new Ultra-Modern church was built in 1982.

Chicago Catholic Churches

TOP **ST. CHARLES BORROMEO**
Legend has it, as documented in a book by former priest Rocco A. Facchini, the church was haunted by the ghost of Bishop Muldoon, who built this church at Roosevelt and Hoyne. The parish itself was established in 1885, and despite the hauntings, or maybe because of them, the church was closed and demolished in 1968.

MIDDLE **ST. CALLISTUS**
Our Lady of Pompeii's Scalabrini order established this small parish at Bowler and Leavitt in 1919. The church and combined school served the mostly Italian community on the western boundaries of Little Italy. The parish status changed in 1994 and is now considered an oratory.

BOTTOM **MATERNITY BVM**
This parish was established in 1909, the church cornerstone was dedicated in 1910 and construction was completed in 1911. This Humboldt Park church is located at North Avenue and Monticello, and in 2018, the parish merged with St. Francis Assisi and St. Philomena to become the parish of San Jose Sanchez del Rio.

A Sketchbook

ST. WILLIAM OF VERCELLI
The Mont Clare neighborhood was nicknamed "Mud Clare" by locals, as there were no paved sidewalks or streets when this parish was established in 1914. After worshiping in a small frame Colonial church and later a brick combined school and church, this classic Mid-Century Modern church was built in 1958 at the corner of Wrightwood and Sayre.

ST. FRANCIS BORGIA
This church, with its dramatically sloped roofline and classic Mid-Century Modern architecture, stands at Addison and Forest Preserve Drive. The parish was established in 1949 to serve veterans of World War II who began to settle in the growing Dunning neighborhood.

TOP
ST. JAMES THE APOSTLE
This parish was established by Polish Catholics in 1914 in the Hanson Park neighborhood. This Georgian Colonial church, designed by architect Chester Tobolski, was built in 1970 at Fullerton and Menard.

BOTTOM
ST. FERDINAND
Architect Gerald W. Barry designed this Mid-Century Art Deco church at Mason and Barry. The parish was established in 1927, and the church was built in 1959.

ST. PRISCILLA
Another prime example of Mid-Century Modernist architecture, this church, at 6949 West Addison, held its first mass on Christmas Eve 1957.

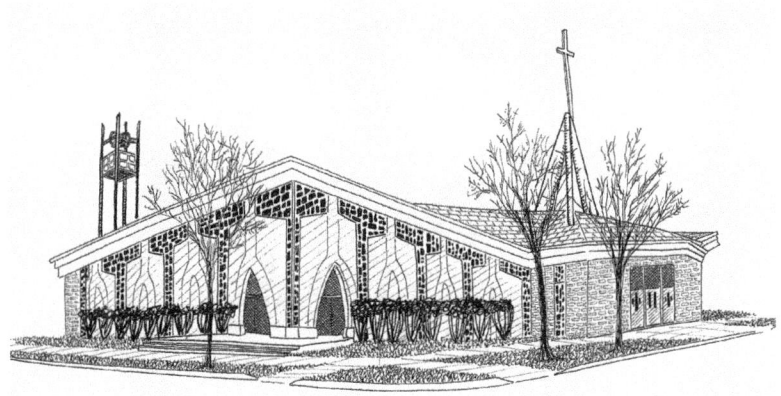

ST. CONSTANCE
Serving Polish Catholics and established in 1916, this Modernist church at Strong and Marmora was built in 1970.

ST. WENCESLAUS
As Avondale grew, so did its Polish Catholic congregation, which established this parish in 1912. This Romanesque church at 3400 North Monticello was built in 1942.

ST. VERONICA
This small parish was established in 1904 by Polish Catholics. This combined church and school's campus is located at the corner of School Street and Whipple and closed in 1991. Today, the structure is home to Concordia Place early years' education.

ST. SYLVESTER
Overlooking Humboldt Boulevard at Palmer Street stands this Victorian Gothic church, built in 1907. The parish was established in 1884 when the land was still part of the Jefferson Township before being annexed into Chicago. Their first masses were held in the firehouse on Stave Street.

TOP **CHRIST THE REDEEMER BELARUSIAN**
From 1955 until its closing in 2003, this was the United States' only Belarusian Greek Catholic church. This Byzantine-inspired church is located at 3107 West Fullerton. Since the archdiocese closed the church, it has been home to the Ss. Peter and Paul Romanian Catholic Church.

BOTTOM **ST. HEDWIG MISSION**
Founded by Polish Catholics in 1939, this tiny frame church at 2445 North Washtenaw is now a private residence, having closed in 1990.

A Sketchbook

OUR LADY OF GRACE
The Logan Square neighborhood established this parish in 1909, and the church was completed in 1911. The yellow brick church is at Altgeld and Ridgeway.

Chicago Catholic Churches

TOP **ST. JOHN BERCHMAN** Belgian Catholics established this parish on their homeland's independence day, September 2, 1905. This Spanish Romanesque church at 2519 West Logan Square Boulevard was built in 1907.

BOTTOM **ST. GENEVIEVE** This parish was founded by Irish Catholics in 1902. This Modern Romanesque church at Altgeld and Lamon was built in 1941.

A Sketchbook

TOP **OUR LADY OF MERCY**
Known for its golden dome high above Albany Park, this church at 4432 North Troy was founded in 1911 and built in 1912. In 2021, the parish merged with St. Edward, Resurrection and Immaculate Heart of Mary.

BOTTOM
ST. HYACINTH MISSION
This former Protestant church at Barry and Spaulding is the home of one of St. Hyacinth's missions, established in 1944.

Chicago Catholic Churches

TOP **ST. MARK** Originally founded by Irish Catholics in the Humboldt Park neighborhood in 1884, this parish saw its parishioners' ethnic makeup change several times. This Mid-Century Modern church was built in 1962 at Thomas and Campbell.

BOTTOM **RESURRECTION** Originally named St. Francis Xavier back in 1888, the parish was officially dissolved in 1991. Resurrection Church at Nelson and Francisco was closed after a merge in 2021.

TOP **ST. FIDELIS**
In 1926, Irish Catholics established this parish and erected a church at 1404 North Washtenaw in 1939. That church was razed in 1968, and the church and school were combined until they both closed in 2006.

MIDDLE **ANNUNCIATION**
This parish began as a mission of St. Columbkille in 1866. This Gothic church at Wabansia and Paulina was closed and razed in 1978.

BOTTOM **ST. HELEN**
This parish was established in 1913, but this Mid-Century church wasn't built until 1965. The architectural firm of Pirola and Erbach designed this Modern Art Deco church at Augusta and Oakley.

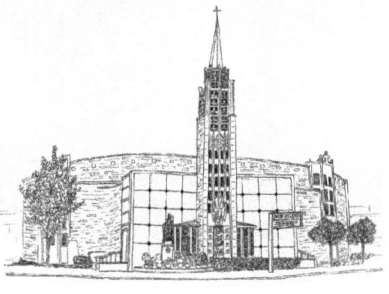

ST. ALOYSIUS
This Mid-Century Modern church at LeMoyne and Claremont was built in 1965. It was the fourth church built for what began as a German parish in 1884.

ST. HYACINTH
In the neighborhood known as Jackawow to the Polish Catholics, this parish was established in 1921. The classic Renaissance church at 3635 West George became a basilica in 2003.

Chicago Catholic Churches

TOP
ST. PHILOMENA
Established by German Catholics in 1894, this Neo-Gothic church at Cortland and Kedvale was built in 1922. The parish was extinguished in 2021 after a merge with Maternity BVM and St. Francis Assisi to become the new San Jose Luis Sanchez del Rio Parish.

BOTTOM
ST. JOHN BOSCO
Salesian followers of St. John "Don" Bosco established this parish in 1934. In 1965, this Mid-Century Modern church by Belli and Belli architects was built at Belden and McVicker.

TOP **ST. LADISLAUS**
Described as simplistic Romanesque, this classic church, designed by architect Leo Strelka, at Long and Henderson, was built in 1955. The parish was established in 1914 as a mission of St. Wenceslaus.

BOTTOM **ST. MARY OF PROVIDENCE**
The church lies within this home for people of diverse abilities at 4200 North Austin. This Spanish Colonial–style brick building was built in 1925.

CHICAGO CATHOLIC CHURCHES

TOP
OUR LADY OF AGNOLA
This Latvian parish was established in 1958 after moving into a former Danish Lutheran church at Rockwell and Wabansia in 1958. The church was closed in 2007.

BOTTOM
ST. STANISLAUS BISHOP AND MARTYR
Originally founded as a mission to St. Stanislaus Kostka, this parish was established in 1893 by Polish Catholic farmers. As the Cragin area developed from rural to residential, this Renaissance church inspired by the Polish Cathedral style was built in 1927 at Belden and Lorel.

A Sketchbook

ST. STANISLAUS KOSTKA
The mother church of all Chicago Polish churches, this Renaissance church at Noble and Greenview was inspired by Polish Cathedral style and is in fact modeled after a cathedral in Krakow. The parish was established in 1867, and the church, designed by noted architect Patrick Keely, was completed in 1881. The south cupola was struck by lightning in 1964 and destroyed.

ST. BONIFACE
Named for the patron saint of Germany, this Romanesque church at Noble and Chestnut was built in 1904. The parish donated the adjacent ten acres to the Chicago Park District and closed in 1990. There have been several recent efforts to save the structure.

HOLY TRINITY
This Renaissance church with Baroque influence at 1120 North Noble Street was built in 1906. The structure originally had an "upper church" and a "lower church" to host masses in both Polish and English. These days, the lower church is called the catacombs and is home to a wide collection of holy relics and stones from locations overseas.

Chicago Catholic Churches

TOP **ST. HEDWIG**
Resurrectionists founded this church in 1888. This Renaissance church, designed by Alphonsus Druiding, was built in 1901 at Hoyne and Webster.

BOTTOM
OUR LADY OF VICTORY
This territorial parish was established in 1906. The lower-level Marion Chapel was built at 5220 West Agatite in 1928, but the upper, Spanish Mission–style structure with Art Deco influences wasn't completely finished until 1954. The parish merged in 2021 to become the new parish of Our Lady of the Rosary.

IMMACULATE HEART OF MARY (NORTH)
This Mid-Century Neo-Modernist church at Byron and Spaulding was built in 1958. The parish, established in 1912, recently closed after a merge with St. Edward and Resurrection.

ST. SEBASTIAN
Established in 1887, this tiny frame church was originally built closer to Halsted Street, but parishioners and engineers physically moved the structure to its current location at 927 West Wellington. The church suffered a fire in 1989 and was closed and razed in 1990.

ST. VINCENT DEPAUL
Legend has it that Reverend Edward Smith built the church after having seen it in a dream. This French Romanesque church at 1004 West Webster was built in 1897, shortly after the parish was founded in 1895. Sadly, the church's visionary never celebrated within, as the very first mass held in the new church was his own funeral.

ST. TERESA
This Old Town parish was established in 1889. A fire destroyed the original church in 1959, and this Mid-Century Modern structure at Armitage and Kenmore was built in 1963.

A Sketchbook

TOP **ST. JOSAPHAT** Originally built to serve Chicago's Polish-Kashubian parishioners who came to Chicago from Prussia, this Romanesque church at 2301 North Southport was built in 1902.

BOTTOM **ST. CLEMENT** Roman emperor Trajan had an anchor tied around Pope St. Clement's neck and threw him into the sea, hence the structure's anchor motif. This Romanesque/Byzantine church at 646 West Deming Place was built in 1918.

Chicago Catholic Churches

TOP **ST. FRANCES XAVIER CABRINI (NATIONAL SHRINE OF)**
Named for the United States' first saint, St. Frances Xavier Cabrini, better known as Mother Cabrini, this shrine stands at 2520 North Lakeview. The shrine was originally built within St. Columbus Hospital, which she founded, worked and died within. But when the hospital was closed and razed in 2012, the shrine, originally designed by architect Leonard Gliatto in 1955, was preserved.

BOTTOM **ST. BONAVENTURE**
St. Bonnie's to locals, this parish was established in 1911 at 1641 West Diversey. The parish's first appointed pastor was a cop turned priest, Father Maguire, who was a constable in Ireland before coming to the United States.

ST. ALPHONSUS
This Gothic church built in 1897 was nearly lost in a fire in 1950. The original plans to rebuild included a smaller flat roof, but they were denied by Cardinal Stritch, who demanded an identical rebuild, albeit this time with steel rafters.

Chicago Catholic Churches

TOP **OUR LADY OF MOUNT CARMEL**
Known as the mother church of the North Shore, this English Gothic church at 700 West Belmont was built in 1914. The Lakeview parish was established in 1886.

BOTTOM **ST. ANDREW**
This North Italian Renaissance church at 3550 North Paulina was built in 1913. The parish was established in 1894 and celebrated its first mass above a nearby tavern. A small frame church was constructed until the present church was built. The church was stretched and nearly doubled in size in the 1930s.

A Sketchbook

ST. BENEDICT
Affectionately known simply as St. Ben's, this Romanesque church at Irving Park Road and Leavitt was built in 1918. Established in 1902, the church and adjacent school fell into financial trouble in the 1990s until a surprise anonymous donation of over $4.5 million assisted in improving conditions and keeping the parish and school open.

Chicago Catholic Churches

TOP **QUEEN OF ANGELS**
Overlooking Welles Park is this Neo-Gothic church, designed by Joseph W. McCarthy and built in 1940. The parish was established in 1909, and the current church is located on the corner of Sunnyside and Claremont.

BOTTOM **ST. MARY OF THE LAKE**
Built in 1917, this Roman Basilica–style church at 4200 North Sheridan has a campanile modeled after St. Pudentiana in Rome. Architect Henry J. Schlacks designed this Buena Park church. During the Cold War, the priests allowed the children from the adjoined grammar school up in the bell tower to watch the D-Day reenactments at Montrose Beach.

OUR LADY OF LOURDES
This Spanish Romanesque church at Leland and Ashland is known as the church that crossed the street. Due to an explosion in development and apartment buildings and the city's plan to widen Ashland Avenue, in 1929, engineers raised the church, originally built in 1916, from its original foundation and moved it across the street—a spectacular feat of modern engineering.

ST. THOMAS CANTERBURY
The columns on the façade of this Joseph W. McCarthy church define its American Neoclassical architecture. The parish was established in 1916, and the church at 4815 North Kenmore was built one year later. The parish merged with St. Ita; however, it is still home to the Greater Chicago Food Depository, feeding the needy in Uptown as it has for generations.

ST. ITA
The only parish named for St. Ita in the United States, this French Gothic church was influenced by the cathedrals of Chartres and Brou in France. Built in 1927 at 5500 North Broadway, it was designed by architect Henry J. Schlacks. The cornerstone is said to have come from the ruins of an ancient Irish monastery.

ST. GERTRUDE
The parish was established in 1911 and planned to build a church. The Depression struck, however, and this English Gothic church at Granville and Greenwood wasn't completed until 1931, thanks to the generosity of the parishioners. In fact, the eucharistic chalice was made from jewelry donated by parishioners during the time.

Selfish employers of labor have flattered the church by calling it the great conservative force, and then called upon it to act as police force while they paid a pittance of wages to those who worked for them. I hope that day is gone by. Our place is beside the poor, behind the working man.
They are the people.

—*Cardinal George Mundelein*

A Sketchbook

TOP **ST. GREGORY**
Cardinal Mundelein called this church a "medieval gem in a modern setting" during its dedication in 1926. This Norman Gothic church is on the corner of Paulina and Bryn Mawr.

BOTTOM **ST. MATTHIAS**
Established by German Catholics in 1887, this church at Ainslie and Claremont was built in 1915. The very first mass was held on Christmas Day.

TOP
MADONNA DELLA STRADA
Built as a chapel for Loyola students, this Modern Art Deco church at 6525 North Sheridan was constructed in 1939. The name of this church is the ancient Latin title for Our Lady of the Way.

BOTTOM
ST. MARGARET MARY
Designed by Joseph W. McCarthy, this Renaissance Revival church at Chase and Claremont was built in 1938. The parish, established in 1921, was consolidated with several West Rogers Park churches to form the new Holy Child Jesus Parish in 2021.

OUR LADY OF THE CROSS MISSION
Established in 1948 as a mission of St. Margaret Mary, this parish was intended to serve those parishioners west of Western Avenue. This Modern church at 2849 West Chase was closed in 1987, razed in 2014 and is now the grounds of the Beis Medresh Mikor Hachaim Jewish synagogue.

ST. HENRY
Established in 1851, this parish was the first Luxembourg Catholic church in Chicago. The original church built in 1906 became part of Angel Guardian after St. Henry's built this combined church and school building at 6335 North Hoyne in 1929.

ST. IGNATIUS
In a neighborhood known to locals as "The Patch," this Roman Renaissance church at 6555 North Glenwood was built in 1917 and closed in 2020.

TOP **ST. TIMOTHY**
This combined church and school at 6330 North Washtenaw was built in 1925. After a merge in 2020, the parish was dissolved.

BOTTOM
ST. JEROME
Known for having the longest aisle in Chicago, this church was stretched and doubled in size in 1934. This North Italian Renaissance structure at 1701 West Lunt was built in 1916 and merged with St. Ignatius and St. Gertrude in 2020..

A Sketchbook

ST. PASCAL
Before construction of this Spanish Mission–style church with Art Deco accents, the parish worshiped in the nearby Pioneer Theatre. Established in 1914 and built that same year, the church is located on Irving Park Road and Melvina Street.

Chicago Catholic Churches

OUR LADY OF MOTHER OF CHURCH
The city's westernmost church, this Mid-Century Modern church at 8747 West Lawrence was built in 1968.

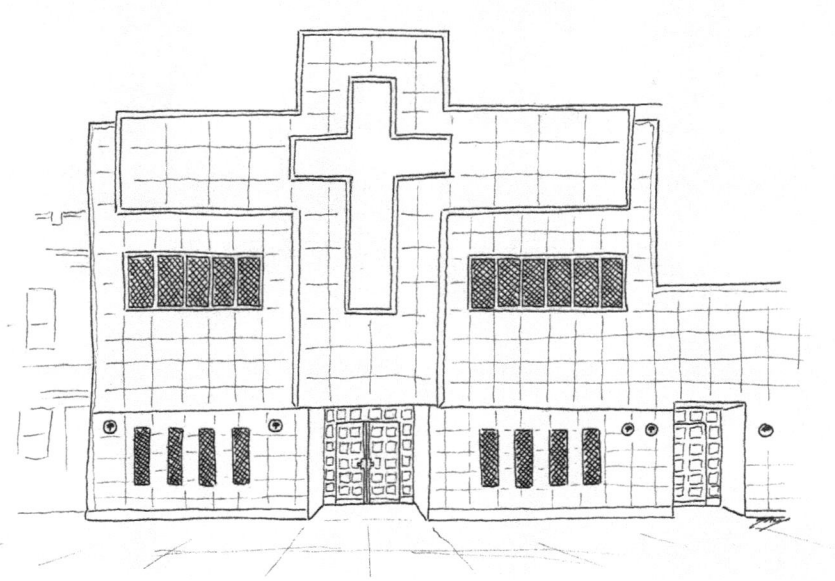

SHRINE OF THE SACRED HEART
Established by Polish Jesuits, this Modern structure at 5835 West Irving Park Road features a giant cross constructed into the façade.

TOP **ST. BARTHOLOMEW**
One of the rare churches built in an American Colonial style, this church at Addison and Lavergne was built in 1938. The parish was established in 1917 on the day of the feast of St. Bartholomew.

BOTTOM **KOREAN MARTYRS CATHOLIC CHURCH**
Recognized by Chicago's Roman Catholic archdiocese, this small American Colonial church is located at 4115 North Kedvale. The name reflects the nearly ten thousand Korean Catholic murder victims of religious persecution in the nineteenth century.

TOP **ST. VIATOR**
The town of Jefferson was home to this parish originally founded in 1888. This Tudor Gothic church at Addison and Kedvale was built in 1929. This parish has the distinction of founding twenty-five additional parishes.

BOTTOM **ST. EDWARD**
Established in 1899, the resilient parishioners began church construction in 1926. The Great Depression slowed down the process, and this Renaissance church at Sunnyside and Kostner wasn't completed until 1940.

ST. EUGENE
The parish was founded in 1948, and a short time later, this Mid-Century Modern church was built at Foster and Canfield.

ST. CORNELIUS
Statues of St. Cornelius and St. Peter flank the stained-glass windows of this Mid-Century Modern church at 5430 West Foster. The parish was established in 1925 and held its masses in Beaubien School. This church was completed in 1965.

TOP **TRANSFIGURATION OF OUR LORD**
Parishioners originally worshiped in Budlong Public School before completing the church in 1912, one year after the parish was established. Polish and Irish immigrant locals called this church at Carmen and Rockwell the "old country church" because of its similarity to the rural churches they were used to. The church was closed in 2020.

BOTTOM **ST. HILARY**
On the property of an old pickle farm, St. Hilary's was established in 1926. The Modern-Romanesque church was built in 1956, and in 2020, the church merged with Transfiguration to create the new parish of St. Padre Pio.

ST. ROBERT BELLARMINE
Carl E. Hundreiser designed this Modern/New Formalist church at Eastwood and Austin. The parish was established in 1930.

ST. MONICA
Established in 1948, this parish worshiped in Garvey School until this Modern church at Foster and Nottingham was built two years later.

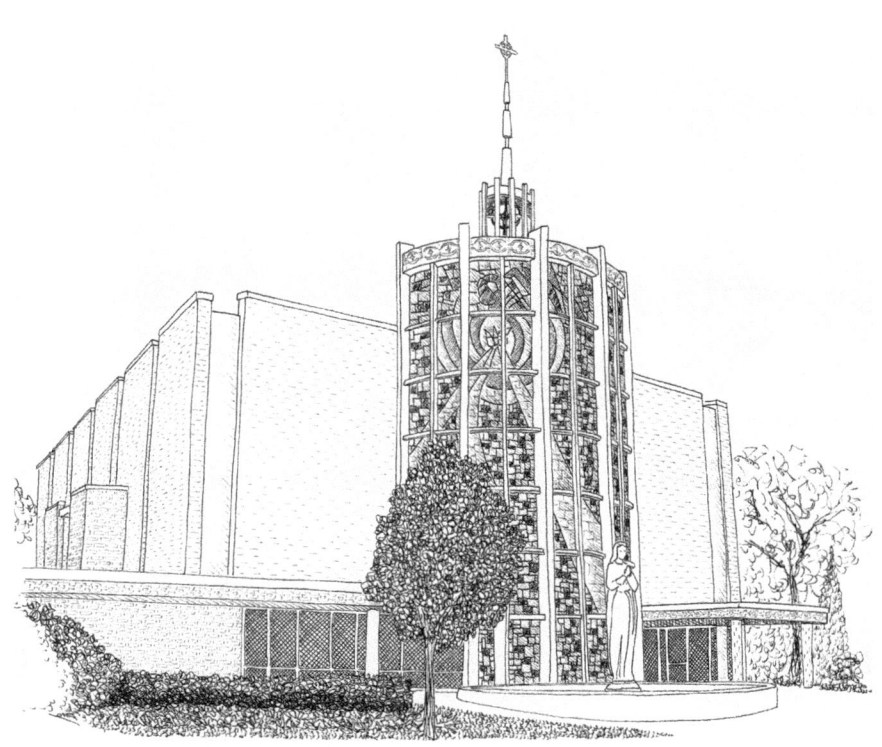

IMMACULATE CONCEPTION
The parish was established in 1911, but this Mid-Century Modern church at 7211 West Talcott wasn't built until 1963. Designed by architect Richard V. Wagener of the Meyer and Cook architectural firm, the impressive structure took three years to build.

ST. TARCISSUS
Built with an Early Modernist design, this church at Ardmore and McVicker held its first mass on Easter Sunday in 1954. The parish was established in 1926.

ST. THECLA
This territorial parish was established in 1925, and this Modernist church at Devon and Oak Park was built in 1962. The parish was closed after a merge with St. Cornelius and St. Tarcissus.

ST. JULIANA
Ebinger School hosted this parish's first masses in 1927. This Neo-Classical church at Touhy and Oketo was built in 1964.

ST. MARY OF THE WOODS
This Mid-Century Modern church at 7033 North Moselle was designed by Gaul and Voosen and was completed in 1953. The parish was established the year prior, and parishioners worshiped in a storefront on Touhy Avenue while waiting for the construction to be completed.

QUEEN OF ALL SAINTS
This impressive Gothic church at 6184 North Sauganash, with a front lawn that stretches to Devon Avenue, was built in 1960. The parish was established in 1929, and the structure was declared a basilica by Pope John XXIII. At the time, it was one of only fourteen in the United States.

I pray that the people of your beautiful city never lose hope, that they work together to become builders of peace, showing future generations the true power of love. I ask you to pray for me too.

—*Pope Francis's letter to Chicago,* From the Vatican, April 4, 2017

BIBLIOGRAPHY

Archdiocese of Illinois archives.

Bochar, Jack. *Locations of Roman Catholic Churches, 1850–1990.* N.p.: Czech and Slovak American Genealogy Society of Illinois, 1997.

Illustrated Souvenir of the Archdiocese of Chicago. *Commemorating the Installation of the Most Reverend Archbishop George W. Mundelein, DD.* February 9, 1916.

Lane, George. *Chicago Churches and Synagogues.* Chicago: Loyola University Press, 1981.

Lindberg, Richard C. *Quotable Chicago.* Chicago: Wild Onion/Loyola University Press, 1996.

INDEX

A

All Saints 90
All Saints (Original) 45
All Saints–St. Anthony 44
Angel Guardian 19
Annunciata 90
Annunciation 145
Assumption 24
Assumption (24th and California) 40
Assumption BVM 68
Assumption BVM (closed) 97

B

Blessed Aloysius Stepinac 19
Blessed Maria Gabriella 112
Blessed Mother Cabrini 127
Blessed Sacrament 40

C

Christ Our Light 99
Christ the King 102
Christ the King Sovereign Priest 71
Christ the Redeemer Belarusian 140
Corpus Christi 61

E

Epiphany 41

F

Five Holy Martyrs 112

G

Good Shepherd 42

H

Haitian Catholic Apostolate 78
Holy Angels 54
Holy Child Jesus Parish 168
Holy Cross 48, 56, 57, 59, 72

Index

Holy Family 114
Holy Ghost 131
Holy Guardian Angel 113
Holy Innocents 112
Holy Name Cathedral 22
Holy Name of Mary 91
Holy Rosary 90, 92, 122
Holy Trinity 124, 153
Holy Trinity (Croatian) 35

I

Immaculate Conception 83, 111, 178
Immaculate Conception (North Park) 30
Immaculate Conception (Original 30
Immaculate Heart of Mary (North) 155
Immaculate Heart of Mary Vicariate 56

J

Jesus Bread of Life 141

K

Korean Martyrs Catholic Church 173

M

Madonna Della Strada 168
Mary, Mother of God 164
Mary, Mother of Mercy 103
Maternity BVM 134
Monastery of the Holy Cross 48
Mother of the Americas 39, 40

N

Nativity BVM 104
Nativity of Our Lord 51
Notre Dame 27

O

Our Lady Gate of Heaven 88
Our Lady Help of Christians 122
Our Lady of Africa 54
Our Lady of Agnola 150
Our Lady of Angels 121
Our Lady of Fatima (North) 53
Our Lady of Fatima (South) 52
Our Lady of Good Counsel 50, 113
Our Lady of Grace 141
Our Lady of Guadalupe 86
Our Lady of Hungary 86
Our Lady of Lourdes 123, 163
Our Lady of Mercy 143
Our Lady of Mother of Church 172
Our Lady of Mount Carmel 160
Our Lady of Nazareth 90
Our Lady of Peace 78
Our Lady of Pompeii 120
Our Lady of Snows 110
Our Lady of Solace 70
Our Lady of Sorrows Basilica 119
Our Lady of Tepeyac 39
Our Lady of the Cross Mission 169
Our Lady of the Gardens 98
Our Lady of the Holy Family 114
Our Lady of the Miraculous Medal 98
Our Lady of the Rosary 154
Our Lady of Victory 154
Our Lady of Vilna 42

Index

P

Precious Blood 126
Presentation 121
Providence of God 34

Q

Queen of All Saints 181
Queen of Angels 162
Queen of Apostles 167
Queen of the Universe 103

R

Resurrection 128, 144

S

Sacred Heart 87, 126
Sacred Heart (Mission of Holy Name of Mary) 91
Sacred Heart of Jesus 59
Sacred Heart (Pilsen) 36
San Jose Luis Sanchez del Rio Parish 148
San Marcello Mission 28
Santa Maria Addolorata 123
Santa Maria Incoronata 42
Shrine of the Sacred Heart 172
Ss. Peter and Paul 52
Ss. Peter and Paul (East) 85
Ss. Peter and Paul (South) 97
St. Adalbert 33
St. Adrian 103
St. Agatha 133
St. Agnes 53
St. Agnes of Bohemia 46
St. Ailbe 84

St. Aloysius (New) 146
St. Aloysius (Old) 146
St. Alphonsus 159
St. Ambrose 59
St. Andrew 160
St. Angela 130
St. Anne 64
St. Anne (Pilsen) 35
St. Anselm 69
St. Anthony 94
St. Augustine 63
St. Barbara 45
St. Barnabas 101
St. Bartholomew 173
St. Basil 63
St. Bede the Venerable 102
St. Benedict 161
St. Benedict the African 72
St. Benedict the African (West) 74
St. Bernard 71
St. Bonaventure 158
St. Boniface 152
St. Brendan 73
St. Bride 76
St. Bridget 47
St. Bronislava 79
St. Bruno 110
St. Cajetan 100
St. Callistus 134
St. Camillus 107
St. Carthage 76
St. Casimir 39
St. Catherine of Genoa 97
St. Cecelia 56
St. Charles Borromeo 134
St. Charles Lwanga 64
St. Christina 100
St. Clara–St. Gelasius 71
St. Clare Montefalco 107

Index

St. Clement 157
St. Clotilde 81
St. Columba 99
St. Columbanus 74
St. Columbkille 127
St. Constance 137
St. Cornelius 175
St. Cyril and Methodius 61, 128
St. Daniel the Prophet 108
St. David 50
St. Denis 103
St. Dominic 29
St. Dorothy 77
St. Edward 174
St. Elizabeth 54
St. Elizabeth of the Trinity 179
St. Ethelreda 84
St. Eugene 175
St. Faustina 108
St. Felicitas 81
St. Ferdinand 136
St. Fidelis 145
St. Finbarr 124
St. Florian 98
St. Frances Xavier Cabrini 127
St. Frances Xavier Cabrini (National Shrine of) 158
St. Francis Assisi (Roosevelt) 123
St. Francis Assisi (West) 128
St. Francis Borgia 135
St. Francis DePaula 77
St. Francis De Sales 89
St. Gabriel 55
St. Gall 106
St. Genevieve 142
St. George 50, 53, 87
St. Gertrude 165
St. Gregory 167
St. Hedwig 154

St. Hedwig Mission 140
St. Helen 145
St. Helena of the Cross 88
St. Henry 169
St. Hilary 176
St. Hyacinth 147
St. Hyacinth Mission 143
St. Ignatius 169
St. Ita 164
St. James 32
St. James Chapel 22
St. James the Apostle 136
St. Jane de Chantel 108
St. Jarlath 120
St. Jerome 170
St. Jerome (Croatian) 47
St. Joachim 85
St. John 33
St. John Baptist 82
St. John Berchman 142
St. John Bosco 148
St. John Cantius 115
St. John De La Salle 89
St. John Fisher 100
St. John Nepoceme 48
St. John of God 66
St. John the Baptist 62
St. Josaphat 157
St. Joseph 29, 82
St. Josephina Bakhita 75
St. Joseph (Pilsen) 34
St. Joseph (Shrine of) 60
St. Joseph/St. Anne 52
St. Juliana 180
St. Justin Martyr 74
St. Katharine of Drexel 84
St. Kevin 89
St. Kilian 82
St. Ladislaus 149

Index

St. Laurence 75
St. Leo the Great 76
St. Louis De France 94
St. Lucia 47
St. Lucy 131
St. Ludmilla 43
St. Malachy 125
St. Margaret Mary 168
St. Margaret of Scotland 101
St. Mark 144
St. Martin 67
St. Martin de Porres 129
St. Mary (Chapel) 21
St. Mary (Colonial) 20
St. Mary Magdalene 81
St. Mary (Modern) 21
St. Mary of Mount Carmel 104
St. Mary of Perpetual Help 49
St. Mary of Providence 149
St. Mary of the Angels 117
St. Mary of the Assumption 20
St. Mary of the Assumption (South) 99
St. Mary of the Lake 162
St. Mary of the Woods 180
St. Mary (Plymouth) 21
St. Mary Star of the Sea 105
St. Matthew 118
St. Matthias 167
St. Maurice 51
St. Mel 132
St. Michael 80
St. Michael (Old Town) 31
St. Michael the Archangel 43
St. Michael the Archangel (South) 60
St. Monica (North) 177
St. Monica (South) 51
St. Moses the Black 81
St. Mother of Teresa of Calcutta 45
St. Nicholas 98

St. Nicholas of Tolentine 106
St. Padre Pio 176
St. Pancratius 111
St. Pascal 171
St. Patrick 87
St. Patrick (Old St. Pat's) 25
St. Paul 37
St. Peter 23
St. Peter Canisius 131
St. Philip Benizi 28
St. Philip Neri 75
St. Philomena 148
St. Pius V 38
St. Priscilla 137
St. Procopius 36
St. Raphael 66
St. Rene Goupil 105
St. Richard 109
St. Rita of Cascia 70
St. Robert Bellarmine 177
St. Roman 43
St. Rose of Lima 59
St. Sabina 77
St. Salomea 95
St. Sebastian 155
St. Simon the Apostle 109
St. Stanislaus Bishop and Martyr 150
St. Stanislaus Kostka 151
St. Stephen 38, 118
St. Stephen King of Hungary 113
St. Sylvester 139
St. Symphorosa and Her Seven Sons 105
St. Tarcissus 179
St. Teresa 156
St. Thaddeus 88
St. Thecla 179
St. Theodore 69
St. Therese Chinese 42

Index

St. Therese of the Infant Jesus 79
St. Thomas Aquinas 129
St. Thomas Canterbury 163
St. Thomas More 102
St. Thomas the Apostle 68
St. Timothy 170
St. Tiribius 106
St. Veronica 138
St. Viator 174
St. Vincent DePaul 156
St. Vitus 39
St. Walter 99
St. Wenceslaus 23, 138
St. William of Vercelli 135
St. Willibrord 91

T

Transfiguration of Our Lord 176
Two Holy Martyrs 105

V

Visitation 65

ABOUT THE AUTHOR

"What parish are ya from?"
That was the typical Chicago Catholic greeting while growing up, living and working in the city. Catholics long identified with their parishes over their neighborhood real estate names.

Harrison Fillmore is the nom de plume of a thirty-five-plus-year city worker and lifelong resident, here in the city of Chicago. The job afforded him the experiences and observations of every neighborhood, every parish and every nook and cranny of this city. He began sketching city scenes at a very early age, and approximately twenty-five years ago, he became inspired after witnessing the demolition of several beautiful churches. Thus, he began a project intending to sketch every single Catholic church in Chicago.

Having grown up Catholic, the author/artist, like many Catholics, grew attachments to several churches during his lifetime. He was baptized in one, communed and confirmed in another and married in yet another. His parents had connections to their old parishes, as did his grandparents before them, reflective of the family histories of many a Chicago Catholic.

The process was a simple one, yet labor intensive. The churches were outlined for scale in pencil and then drawn freehand in pen-and-ink. Some of the more ornate churches would take hours, even days. The results are realistic illustrations intended to spark one's own memories of their respective churches.

Visit us at
www.historypress.com

www.ingramcontent.com/pod-product-compliance
Lightning Source LLC
Chambersburg PA
CBHW070356100426
42812CB00005B/1531